COCKTAIL NOIR

COCKTAIL NOIR

FROM GANGSTERS AND GIN JOINTS TO GUMSHOES AND GIMLETS

SCOTT M. DEITCHE

BEIJING MEDIATIME BOOKS CO., LTD.
Reservoir Square Books, Inc.
100 Jericho Quadrangle, Suite 337
Jericho, NY 11753
cntimesbooks.com

Ordering Information
Quantity sales: Special discounts are available on quantity purchases by corporations, associations, and others. For details, contact the publisher at the address above.
Orders by U.S. trade bookstores and wholesalers: Please contact Ingram Publisher Services:
Tel: (866) 400-5351; Fax: (800) 838-1149; or customer.service@ingrampublisherservices.com.

ISBN 978-1-94194-700-5

Printed in the United States of America

"Do you drink?"
"Of course, I just said I was a writer."
STEPHEN KING

"I like liquor and women and chess and a few other things."
PHILIP MARLOWE

"Bars and restaurants with liquor licenses are very important to the criminal activities of La Cosa Nostra."
NEW JERSEY STATE COMMISSION OF INVESTIGATION, 1995

The love affair between drink and the written word has endured for centuries. Its images are iconic—the tormented artist seeking salvation in a bottle; the scribe finding his muse in a glass; a crook-backed wordsmith crouched over a keyboard, alternating sentences and swigs. Nowhere is that relationship more evident than in the dark corner of the literary world we call noir, where the passion for booze inevitably seeps into the lives of a writer's characters. The relationship between organized crime and liquor doesn't go back quite as far, but it's just as defining. During Prohibition the mob gained the power it needed to continue running crime in America for over eighty years. Now, from the speakeasies where novelists got their inspiration for famous private eyes and crusading cops, and journalists began chronicling America's fascination with the Mafia, comes *Cocktail Noir*, celebrating the favorite drinks of crime writers and their creations, and of underworld figures both imagined and real.

CONTENTS

Chapter 5 Cocktail Noir on Screen

Whether bantering, scheming, seducing—or doing some combination of the three—celluloid private eyes, gangsters, and femme fatales seem to nearly always have a glass in hand. What's in that glass says a lot about a character. 77

Chapter 6 Real-Life Gangsters

Mobsters love cocktails. They prefer the classics (Manhattans, martinis). They order by brand (Cutty Sark, Dewar's). They want their drinks free, and they want to spend a lot of money on them. Straws? Fuggedaboutit. Cracking the wiseguy bar code. 101

Chapter 7 Gangster Bars

Mobsters have owned, operated, and plotted crimes at hundreds of drinking establishments across the country, many of which are still popular. Some are cashing in on the retro cocktail movement and playing up their gangster history. 131

Chapter 8 Bar Noir

From journalists who cover the crime beat to celebrated novelists, writers have made the bar their second office. A tour through the best of these watering holes—some still serving, some long past last call—shows where writers have always gone for inspiration, company and a good, strong drink. 193

Chapter 9 The Well-Stocked Home Bar

A great cocktail starts with the right ingredients. Here's what every amateur bartender needs to mix drinks like the pros. 217

Acknowledgements 225
References 227
Index 237

INTRODUCTION

I still remember my first real cocktail—not the Everclear punch at Eckerd College parties, not the vodka shooters, not the sugary concoctions endemic to nightclubs, concert venues and college bars—but a true, grown-up's cocktail. It was a martini, made with gin (the *only* way to make a martini, though, as I will cover in this book, other, misguided, notions on this exist). Bombay Sapphire gin, strong yet fragrant. Part of the allure was the sophistication of even ordering the drink. But the flavor, far more complex and appealing than anything I'd tasted before, was what really drew me in. That was my initiation into the cocktail world (as well as my start as a gin drinker).

I can recall just as vividly how, years earlier, I became fascinated with organized crime. My mother was a big fan of mob stories, her interest sparked by the old *Untouchables* TV show with Robert Stack. I grew up watching gangster movies on TV. The small screen also brought real-life mobsters into our home. Living in North Central New Jersey, we got our news from New York City stations. I remember sitting at the kitchen table eating dinner with my family

The *Cocktail Noir* cocktail. Benedictine and Maraschino Liqueur are two key ingredients in the Cocktail Noir. While not always easy to find, these two liqueurs are worth the search. Photo credit: Sari Deitche.

when Eyewitness News broke the Paul Castellano hit. The brazen shooting of the Gambino crime family boss, right before Christmas 1985 on a busy New York street, was the top news story for days and further stoked my curiosity about the underworld.

Five years later, seeing *Goodfellas* on the big screen pushed my interest in organized crime into an obsession. Over the next decade, I read and researched organized crime around the country, contributing pieces to nascent websites that followed mob news. After moving to St. Petersburg, Florida, I wrote my first book, *Cigar City Mafia*, about the Tampa mob. From there I have expanded from writing about gangsters to talking about them on TV and radio, and leading walking tours of mob haunts in Tampa.

Cocktail Noir fuses these two passions of mine. Or maybe it would be more accurate to say that it allows me to explore two interests that were already fused, as well as broaden my focus beyond gangsters to include other disreputable characters. In addition to looking at the intersection of crime and cocktails, I take readers on a tour of the best gangster bars and writer bars across the country. And, naturally, I include recipes for classic cocktails you can create at home or order at your favorite watering hole. Disreputable characters optional.

COCKTAIL NOIR

2 oz. Templeton Rye
½ oz. Benedictine
¼ oz. Maraschino liqueur
3–4 dashes blood orange bitters
Add ingredients to mixing glass with ice. Stir vigorously for 30 seconds. Strain into cocktail glass. Garnish with an orange peel.

THE *COCKTAIL NOIR* COCKTAIL

I developed this signature cocktail for the book, keeping two things in mind. First, I am not a professional mixologist. So I built on simple blocks, nothing too fancy, though two of the ingredients are a little less common. Second, I wanted a drink that would convey the feel of the book. So I chose a rye base, because whiskey is the drink of Prohibition, of cynical PIs, of hardboiled writers, of gangsters, and of shady and mysterious characters and bars. I chose Templeton Rye, Al Capone's favorite. I chose Benedictine because it brings a robust, unique flavor and a classic pedigree. I added a little Maraschino liqueur for flavor, and I added bitters. But not just any bitters. I used blood orange bitters. Because, well, blood.

CHAPTER 1

The Dark Corner with Cocktail in Hand

People in the United States are finally becoming aware that
it's not how much you drink, it's the quality.

MIXOLOGIST KEITH BAKER

What is noir? Google it and the first definition that comes up reads, "A genre of crime film or fiction characterized by cynicism, fatalism, and moral ambiguity." Modern noir aficionado Eddie Muller described it as, "people know they're doing the wrong thing and they do it anyway." While purists may quibble about what does and doesn't fit within the parameters of a noir, I prefer Muller's more expansive definition.

The elements of a *classic* noir novel or film are a convoluted mystery, a femme fatale, wiseguys, PIs, cops, and generally shady characters. Tying those elements together is the intangible feel of noir. You know a noir when you see or read one. You recognize the pulpy feel of the story, the angular camerawork and dark alleys of a film noir. You know the way the characters behave, what they eat.

And, most importantly, what they drink. Noir characters order martinis, gimlets, and brown liquor served straight. They can't pronounce *appletini*.

But noir extends beyond the novel and screen into the real world. Celluloid gangsters, and the lawmen and reporters who chased them, were inspired by their true-life counterparts. The real underworld is as full as fiction of interesting characters, if not more. These gangsters, about which you will read a lot in this book, personify Muller's description of noir—people who knowingly do the wrong thing.

As for fiction, while noir has a decidedly retro appeal, the recent trend of "neo noir" is not so much a return to the past as it is the taking of the visual and dialogue elements of noir and placing them in a modern setting.

Neo noir's influence in modern cinema can be seen in the work of filmmakers from the Coen brothers to Christopher Nolan. *Fargo*, for all its quirky charms, is as much a noir as 1947's *Out of the Past*, a classic of the genre. The dreamscape of Nolan's *Inception* echoes great mid-century noirs like *Kiss Me Deadly*.

The word *cocktail*, like noir, describes something seemingly basic that on closer look has almost infinite variations.

A cocktail is any mixture of a spirit (or spirits) and one or more other ingredient. It can be as simple as a martini or scotch and soda, or as complex as a Zombie. Cocktails span the range from sweet to bitter and every taste in between. There are earthy cocktails and salty cocktails. Ideally, each is as individual as the person imbibing it.

Las Vegas bartender Keith Baker, winner of the Mob Museum's inaugural Boss of the Bars competition. Photo credit: Keith Baker.

"The secret to a great cocktail isn't so much a secret; it has to have balance between the hot liquor flavor, the sweetness, and the bitterness. Delving deeper you have to figure out your guest's levels on these," said Las Vegas mixologist Keith Baker. "For instance, a sweet cocktail to me would taste hot to most people because I make drinks for myself very liquor forward and consider bourbon to be very sweet, while most people would consider it to be a very tough drink. When making cocktails, I ask questions to determine what each person's levels are to the best of my ability and then choose which cocktail I make or change the ratios around for that guest."

Like noir, classic cocktails are an old pleasure that now feels thoroughly modern.

"We've rediscovered so many classics and books that have provided the recipes and ingredients, like crème de violette, so we can experience those drinks first hand, not just read about them," said spirits author Kara Newman. "At the same time, bartenders have invented a canon of new classics. It's hard to characterize a decade-long evolution as just a fad."

"There were always small pockets of cocktail culture. But real seeds started developing in the eighties and nineties. In the last ten years things have really taken off," said Derek Brown, owner of multiple bars in the Washington, DC area. "Cocktails have again become a huge part of the culinary world and it's reinforced what bartending means."

The classics never really disappeared from American bars, Baker said, "they were just being made badly. These recipes are the base of every cocktail you will ever have. After Prohibition there weren't a lot of good bartenders around because no one had been trained in the classic style, and it got worse, culminating in the shit-show that was the eighties. Basically, bartenders were using pre-made, cheap ingredients instead of fresh and, adding way too many ingredients to cover up the crappy taste, made them sweet and tall. They also didn't understand the basics so they had no idea how to map out a cocktail and started dumping flavors in until they worked."

So why this embrace of real cocktails? Why now? Some credit the *Mad Men* effect. Who wouldn't want to look as cool as Don Draper knocking back an Old Fashioned? But this is bigger than a single television show. And it's not a hipster trend. It's part of a larger turn away from prizing quantity and convenience above all else.

"People in the United States are finally becoming aware that it's not how much you drink, it's the quality," Baker said. "The 1960s, 1970s pretty much cemented in the brains of most of us that cheap, microwavable or fast food was the way to go and that mentality carried over into cocktails and beer. The food revolution took off first and mom and pop were now becoming foodies. It was a natural progression for beverages to follow suit."

One of the most influential figures in the rise of cocktail culture is Dale DeGroff, a mixologist who reintroduced many forgotten drinks back into the mainstream. DeGroff is a James Beard Award winner, author of *The Essential Cocktail* and *The Craft of the Cocktail,* and founder of the Museum of the American Cocktail in New Orleans.

Dale DeGroff has a few favorite cocktails. "I drink a Beefeater gin martini with an olive and a twist . . . Having said that, if I am in New Orleans I am drinking Sazeracs . . . if I am at the Buena Vista in San Francisco I am drinking Irish Coffees . . . well you get the idea . . ."

"There are several things that have come together over the last twenty-five years that have impacted the cocktail. The first was the culinary revolution. . . . We changed the way we dine in this country, and beyond our shores similar changes were taking place on a larger scale," DeGroff said. "We fell in love with big flavor. . .ethnic and regional influences combined with classic French, classic Chinese, and fusion cuisine changed the landscape for the diner. Fresh and seasonal became the driving force and people expected that and when faced with artificial mixes and shortcuts at the bar they pushed back."

DeGroff's own biggest influence was his former boss and mentor, Joe Baum, the visionary restauranteur who died in 1998. Baum's New York City establishments, including The Four Seasons in the Seagram Building and La Fonda Del Sol in the Time-Life Building, were standard bearers for seasonal and artisanal ingredients during a time when it was easier to reach for highly processed food, even in restaurants. Baum's approach extended from the kitchen to the bar.

"Joe's cocktail menu in 1959 had three Mezcal drinks, tequila drinks, even a Pisco Sour. Joe demanded a return to classic recipes and only fresh ingredients," DeGroff said.

Many of these classic cocktails called for esoteric and not widely available ingredients. Some absent from US bars for decades were reintroduced as aficionados began asking for these "long lost" bottles. Jason Wilson's book *Boozehound* (a dog-eared copy is always nearby when I'm mixing cocktails) is subtitled *On the Trail of the Rare, the Obscure, and the Overrated in Spirits* and uncovers many ingredients that essentially disappeared during Prohibition and are now not only making a comeback but exceeding their original popularity.

Campari

Some spirits that were always available but had fallen out of favor have surged in popularity. The best example is Campari, a delightfully bitter orange 150-year-old liqueur from Italy and the main ingredient in my favorite cocktail, the Negroni.

Campari representative David Karraker credits the spirit's recent boom to the broader acceptance of the flavor of bitter, particularly in the US, where tastes have long run to the salty, sweet, and savory. Thank the ubiquity of Starbucks coffee, which many perceive as bitter (in a good way), and the rise of specialty grocers for the change.

"Consumers were introduced to a wider variety of foods and beverages thanks to Whole Foods, Trader Joe's, and local farmer's mar-

The Negroni. This bitter-tinged mix of gin, Campari, and sweet vermouth is my favorite cocktail. Photo credit: Campari.

kets," said Karraker. "In the 1970s, kale was relegated to nurturing pet rabbits and could be found only at feed stores. In the 1980s, if mom put Brussels sprouts on your plate, they had a better chance of ending up in the dog's mouth than yours. Today, these two bitter veggies, in addition to radicchio, can be found on every menu. At the bar, hoppy, bitter IPA is the hottest beer going."

THE NEGRONI

1½ oz. gin (my favorites to use here are Hendrick's, Bombay Sapphire, and Death's Door for a heavier juniper punch)
1½ oz. Campari
1½ oz. sweet vermouth
Orange twist

Combine the first three ingredients in a cocktail shaker with ice. Stir and strain into a chilled cocktail glass, garnish with the orange twist.

The Negroni

I first tasted this bittersweet concoction about a decade ago, unsure of how I would like it. I was just getting into more complex and sophisticated cocktails. But with the first sip of the bitter orange spirit combined with sweet vermouth and a bright and aromatic gin, I was a convert. Though it took a few more well-made examples to enshrine the Negroni at the top of my cocktail pyramid, I immediately recognized the drink as something altogether different.

The drink was invented in 1920 at the Café Giacosa in Florence when the Florentine Count Camilio Negroni had the bartender, Fosco Scarselli, substitute gin in an Americano (sweet vermouth, Campari, soda water). Or so the legend goes. Origins of drinks are often difficult to trace, as so many variations on simple mixes weave in and out of cocktail books, bar lore, and urban legend. Many bartenders cling tight to recipes, only to have them recreated elsewhere with a slight variation—and *voilà!* A new cocktail.

THE BOULEVARDIER

1½ oz. bourbon
1½ oz. Campari
1½ oz. sweet vermouth
Orange twist
Combine the first three ingredients in a cocktail shaker with ice. Stir and strain into a chilled cocktail glass. Garnish with the orange twist.

Whatever its origin, I'm far from the first writer to embrace the Negroni. The cocktail appears in two James Bond books. In the short story "Risico," Bond orders a Negroni with Gordon's Gin. In *Thunderball,* he mixes his own Negroni.

"James Bond was a big fan of Campari. It is the first drink ordered in the novel *Casino Royale*, in the form of the Americano. Of course, you can't forget that Ernest Hemingway was also a fan of the Negroni and mentioned it in *Across the River and Into the Trees*," said Karraker. "One of my favorite quotes from Orson Welles after first trying the Negroni: 'The bitters are excellent for your liver. The gin is bad for you. They balance each other.'"

The Boulevardier

A few years ago, I made the rounds of some cocktail bars in Las Vegas. I had an afternoon to go exploring and before heading over to Frankie's Tiki Room (more on that in another chapter), I found myself teaching three bartenders about the Boulevardier, the lesser-known, American-born cousin of the Negroni. The best way to frame the relationship between the Negroni and Boulevardier: The Negroni is spring and summer; the Boulevardier is winter and fall.

The Boulevardier, named after a political satire magazine, was created in Paris in the 1920s by an American who missed the bourbon of his home country.

APEROL NEGRONI

The Aperol in a modified Negroni works well with a dry gin.

1½ oz. dry gin
1½ oz. sweet vermouth
1½ oz. Aperol

Combine the first three ingredients in a cocktail shaker with ice. Stir and strain into a chilled cocktail glass, garnish with an orange twist.

BLACK NEGRONI

The black in the black Negroni is provided by Amaro, an Italian digestif designed for after-dinner drinking. Usually made with a variety of herbs, Amaro is generally a darker and heavier liqueur than Campari. This recipe also adds a couple dashes of orange bitters.

1½ oz. gin
1½ oz. Amaro
1½ oz. Campari
2 dashes orange bitters

Combine the ingredients in a mixing glass with ice. Stir and strain into a chilled cocktail glass, garnish with an orange twist.

Variations

The Negroni and Boulevardier open themselves up to various interpretations.

Aperol Negroni

If Campari is just too bitter for your palate, try using Aperol as a substitute. It still has a tinge of the bitter edge, but it's sweeter and more floral, allowing the orange flavor to shine through.

You can also drink Aperol straight as an aperitif or pair it with Prosecco for an Aperol Spritz. Created to be sipped on sunny, warm European days, an Aperol Spritz is the opposite of a dark, noirish cocktail. But even private eyes and femme fatales need something to drink in the daylight.

LUCIEN GAUDIN

Another variation, named after a legendary French fencer, replaces the sweet vermouth with dry vermouth, and adds another orange-flavored liqueur, Cointreau, to the mix.

1 oz. gin
½ oz. Campari
½ oz. dry vermouth
½ oz. Cointreau
Orange twist

Combine the first four ingredients in a mixing glass with ice. Stir and strain into a chilled cocktail glass, garnish with the orange twist.

The Martini

Few cocktails loom as large in noir, both with the authors and their creations, as the martini. In its purest form, a martini is a straightforward drink: gin (or vodka, if you must), dry vermouth, ice, and an olive or lemon twist. It has a flavorful aroma, especially if you use a gin with a heavily floral bouquet. It goes down easy, which only adds to its allure, and has an air of sophistication about it. A martini is made to be consumed wearing a suit and tie, or at least something more polished than a T-shirt and flip-flops.

Irish Whiskey: Simply put, it's whiskey distilled and aged in Ireland. The specifics that govern whether a spirit is called Irish whiskey were outlined first in the Irish Whiskey Act of 1950, then updated in the Irish Whiskey Act of 1980. The 1980 Act states that whiskey can only be called Irish whiskey if it meets a number of criteria, including that it be distilled in either the Republic of Ireland or Northern Ireland.

EEYORE'S REQUIEM

This modern variation of the Negroni was developed by Chicago mixologist Toby Maloney. It is a far more bitter drink even than the regular Negroni, with Campari acting as the base spirit that the other spirits play against.

1½ oz. Campari
1 oz. Dolin Blanc
½ oz. gin
¼ oz. Cynar
Orange twist

Combine the first four ingredients in a mixing glass with ice. Stir and strain into a chilled cocktail glass, garnish with the orange twist.

The ties between literary figures and the martini are numerous and deep. In the 1920s, writers like F. Scott Fitzgerald and Dorothy Parker—"I like to have a martini, two at the very most. After three I'm under the table, after four I'm under my host"—brought the libation to a whole new audience and exponentially increased its popularity (since this was the era of Prohibition, it didn't hurt that distilling gin was relatively easy).

In the 1950s, Truman Capote espoused the literary virtues of writing with glass in hand: "As the afternoon wears on, I shift from coffee to mint tea to sherry to martinis."

A precursor to the martini debuted in 1862 at San Francisco's Occidental Hotel. It was named after the nearby town of Martinez. The Martinez first appeared in print twenty-five years later in *The Bar-Tender's Guide or How to Mix All Kinds of Plain and Fancy Drinks* by Jerry Thomas.

But it was a later book, 1896's *Stuart's Fancy Drinks and How to Make Them*, that first featured a cocktail closely resembling the modern martini. The book's author, Thomas Stuart, called it a Marguerite.

By the start of the twentieth century, the word *martini* was in regular use by bartenders on both sides of the Atlantic. In his 1934 work, *1700 Cocktails for the Man Behind the Bar*, Robert de Fleury lists five common martini recipes from dry to sweet. That same year saw the publication of *The Thin Man*, in which Dashiell Hammett's comedic noir detectives Nick and Nora Charles banter over, among other things, how to make a martini. Nick opines, "The important thing is the rhythm. Always have rhythm in your shaking. Now a Manhattan you shake to foxtrot time, a Bronx to two-step time, but a dry martini you always shake to waltz time."

By far the most famous literary martini, the one that brought the drink to the attention of the masses, was the one ordered by James Bond in the 1953 novel *Casino Royale*, the first Bond book. Though neither noir nor

MARTINEZ COCKTAIL

(Use small bar-glass.)

1 dash of Boker's bitters
2 dashes of maraschino
1 pony of Old Tom gin
1 wine-glass of vermouth
2 small lumps of ice

Shake thoroughly and strain into a large cocktail glass. Put a quarter of a slice of lemon in the glass and serve. If the guest prefers it very sweet, add two dashes of gum syrup.

MARGUERITE COCKTAIL

1 dash orange bitters
40 mL Plymouth gin
20 mL French vermouth

Stir over ice. Strain into a cocktail glass. Garnish with a cherry and squeeze a lemon twist on top.

VESPER MARTINI

1½ oz. gin
½ oz. vodka
¼ oz. Lillet Blanc
Add to a cocktail shaker with ice. Shake vigorously. Strain into cocktail glass. Garnish with a lemon (or orange) peel.

SLOW MOTION

2 oz. rum
1 oz. Parma
2 oz. orange juice
1 oz. pineapple juice
1 tsp. grenadine
Splash of club soda
Mix in a shaker with ice. Shake well and strain into Collins glass with ice. Garnish with orange peel and a cherry.

hardboiled detective fiction in the purest sense, the Bond novels did retain some of the genres' trappings, especially when it came to libations, femme fatales (Bond girls), and larger-than-life villains.

Bond says to the bartender, "Three measures of Gordon's, one of vodka, half a measure of Kina Lillet. Shake it very well until it's ice-cold, and then add a large thin slice of lemon peel. Got it?"

The Vesper martini, as this drink was known, is believed to be one of the first examples in print of vodka used in a martini. Since then, vodka has (regrettably) overtaken gin as the most frequently used ingredient in a martini. Ian Fleming reportedly got the idea to feature a Vesper martini while drinking one in Dukes Bar in London. Nowadays, visitors to the bar can sip on a Fleming 89, a dessert-like drink created to celebrate the ties between this venerable drinking establishment and the most famous cocktail in literature.

I pause here to note that, with all respect to Mr. Charles and Mr. Bond, a martini should be stirred, not shaken. And it should never, ever be made with vodka. If it's not gin, it's not a martini.

And don't even get me started on appletinis. . . .

More 1940s Cocktails

Many post–Prohibition era drinks that remained in fashion into the 1940s were imbibed by authors, gangsters, and their literary counterparts. The Sloe Gin Fizz and the Stork Club Cooler were two of the most popular.

SLOE GIN FIZZ

1 oz. gin
1 oz. sloe gin
1 oz. lemon juice
1 oz. simple syrup
Dash of club soda

Mix first four ingredients in a cocktail shaker with ice. Shake and strain into a highball glass with ice. Top with club soda.

STORK CLUB COOLER

This cocktail comes from the Stork Club, a famous New York nightclub popular with everyone from politicians to movie stars to gangsters.

2 oz. gin
1 tsp. sugar
Juice of half orange

Mix, shake, and strain into Collins glass with ice. Garnish with fruit.

The El Dorado, a Prohibition-era casino in Tampa. The El Dorado was operated by Charlie Wall, early underworld kingpin of the Cigar City. Photo credit: Burgert Brothers Collection.

CHAPTER 2

Prohibition

From 1919 to 1933 bartending was illegal [in the US]. In that time, you lost a whole generation of bartenders who knew the techniques and the recipes.

DEREK BROWN, WASHINGTON, DC BAR OWNER

January 17, 1920 was the day that changed America forever. That day, the Eighteenth Amendment, also known as the Volstead Act or Prohibition, became the law of the land. Buoyed by a temperance movement that had started decades earlier, some states and local governments were already moving toward curbing alcohol use. But the Eighteenth Amendment took that a step further, banning all production and consumption of alcohol for recreational purposes (leaving a loophole for medicinal production and use by prescription from a doctor).

While some Americans were ready to give up their drinks for fear of law enforcement, many others willingly risked a run-in with police for the sake of a cocktail or beer. The term "speakeasy" became part of the American vernacular, used to describe the underground bars that could only be accessed through passwords and having the right connections to get inside.

Cocktails changed with Prohibition. Recipes were tweaked and altered; some to hide the taste of the rotgut liquor used as a base, others to make use of more available, legal ingredients. This ill-fated attempt to legislate American habits left another legacy, explained Washington, DC bar owner Derek Brown: "There were so many great bartenders with great recipes. The most skilled moved overseas or found new jobs. From 1919 to 1933 bartending was illegal [in the US]. In that time, you lost a whole generation of bartenders who knew the techniques and the recipes."

An illegal still operation in Tampa, Florida. Many of these operations produced rum from cane sugar shipped into Tampa via Cuba. Photo credit: author collection.

As the art of bartending waned, another pursuit flourished. Prohibition is often credited with giving birth to organized crime in America. In truth, organized crime already existed in the ethnic enclaves of big cities and in small, rural towns. There were organized criminals who made money on extorting businesses, running gambling and prostitution, and dealing drugs. But Prohibition launched organized crime into a nationwide phenomenon. It not only allowed criminal gangs to exploit their knack for providing vice to willing customers, it also put them in bed with politicians and law enforcement officials who willingly accepted bribes to look the other way. That led to the institutional corruption that enabled the mob to flourish.

Rum

No spirit was more intertwined with smuggling during Prohibition than rum. In fact, the term *rum-runner* came to envelop all liquor smugglers during Prohibition, even the ones who were bringing whiskey across the Great Lakes. Rum was mainly smuggled into the United States through the Gulf Coast and South Florida. Cuba was the way station, as well as the source for raw materials used in illicit alcohol production—molasses and cane sugar. Through strategic alliances, the mob was able to flood the US with this tropical spirit, inadvertently handing rum companies scores of new customers who helped drive its popularity after Prohibition through the post-WWII years and the tiki craze.

TWELVE MILES OUT

1 oz. rum
1 oz. Calvados
1 oz. Swedish Punsch
Pour ingredients in mixing glass with ice cubes. Stir for 30 seconds. Strain into cocktail glass. Add orange twist for garnish.

TWELVE MILE LIMIT

Not to be confused with the Twelve Miles Out, the long-forgotten Twelve Mile Limit was resurrected in author Ted Haigh's 2009 collection, *Vintage Spirits and Forgotten Cocktails.*

1 oz. white rum
½ oz. whiskey
½ oz. brandy
½ oz. grenadine
½ oz. fresh lemon juice
Add ingredients in a mixing glass with ice. Stir and strain into a (well-chilled) cocktail glass. Garnish with a lemon twist.

Rum Cocktails

One of the lesser-known pieces of the Volstead Act was the ban on consumption of alcohol up to twelve miles offshore (extended from the original limit of three miles—more on that later). This gave many would-be mariners an excuse for heading off on boats designed specifically to shuttle imbibers off the coast. It was, in a sense, the first booze cruise. However, personal boat ownership was nowhere near what it is today, so many drinkers could only imagine what it would be like bobbing in the ocean while drinking illicit rum. Creative bartenders made up a drink for just such an occasion, the aptly named Twelve Miles Out.

This is a relatively simple drink, but the type of rum used can change the flavor dramatically. White rums give the drink a more summertime air, while darker rums add heft and an intriguing flavor profile. The drink also includes two less well-known ingredi-

THREE MILE LIMIT

The Three Mile Limit (which later morphed into the Three-Miler) is a rum and brandy concoction with a dash of grenadine and lemon juice. This was the first of the "middle finger to the feds" drinks that popped up as the booze cruises began sailing.

⅓ oz. rum
⅔ oz. brandy
1 tsp. grenadine
1 tsp. lemon juice

Add ingredients to a cocktail shaker with ice. Shake well and strain into small cocktail glass.

MARY PICKFORD

Named after the famous actress of the silent movie era, the Pickford was created by Eddie Woelke, an American bartender who moved to Havana during Prohibition.

2 oz. rum
1 oz. pineapple juice
1 tsp. grenadine
1 tsp. maraschino cherry liqueur
Maraschino cherry

Add all ingredients to cocktail shaker with ice. Shake and strain into chilled cocktail glass.

EL PRESIDENTE

Woelke also developed this well-known Prohibition-era cocktail at the Sevilla Biltmore in Havana. Years later the Sevilla was part of a network of hotels and casinos owned and operated by the Mafia.

1½ oz. Cana Brava Rum
½ oz. Cointreau
½ oz. dry vermouth
1 dash grenadine
Orange peel

Stir first four ingredients with ice in a cocktail shaker. Shake, then strain into a chilled cocktail glass and garnish with an orange peel.

BETWEEN THE SHEETS

¾ oz. white rum
¾ oz. brandy
¾ oz. triple sec
½ oz. lemon juice
Lemon twist

Stir first four ingredients with ice in a cocktail shaker. Shake, then strain into a chilled cocktail glass and garnish with a lemon peel.

ents, Calvados, an apple brandy, and Swedish Punsch, a rum-based liqueur with various spices. Prohibition was credited with killing off the presence of Punsch in America. Though the bootleggers were running back and forth across the Atlantic, they concentrated on whiskey, an easy seller. Underworld economics did not allow for more esoteric liqueurs like Punsch to make it across. In fact, only recently has Punsch become available again, though you can find many recipes online to make it yourself.

A collection of recipes for Prohibition-era cocktails appears in the following pages.

SIDECAR

The Sidecar is one of the original sour cocktails. Depending on which story you prefer, the drink was either invented in Paris during WWI by a man who regularly rode to the bar in a motorcycle sidecar or by a London bartender Pat MacGarry, a legend in mixology.

1½ oz. cognac

1 oz. Cointreau, triple sec, or other orange liqueur

1 oz. lemon juice

Pour ingredients into cocktail shaker with ice cubes. Shake. Strain into cocktail glass. Add a lemon peel for garnish. Some recipes call for adding sugar to the rim of the glass.

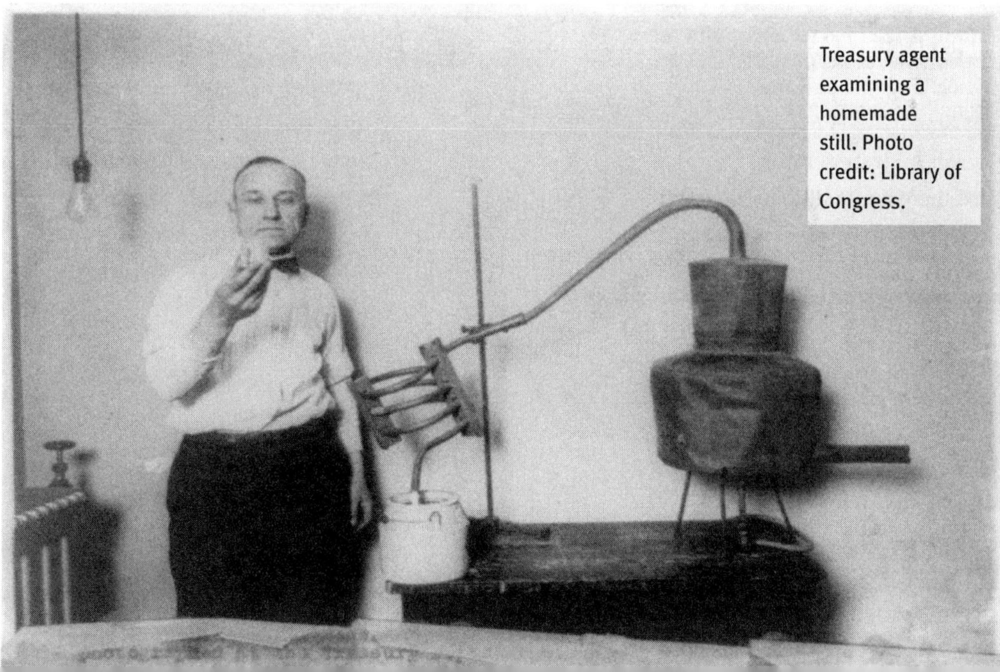

Treasury agent examining a homemade still. Photo credit: Library of Congress.

SOUTHSIDE

The Southside was a popular Prohibition-era cocktail with origins dating back to the late 1800s. Though one origin tale centers on Chicago and Capone, in reality this drink was created at the Southside Sportsmans Club on Long Island.

2 oz. gin

1 oz. lime juice

¾ oz. simple syrup

Mint leaf

Combine gin, lime juice, simple syrup, and mint leaf in a cocktail shaker with ice. Shake vigorously and strain into chilled glass.

DUBONNET COCKTAIL

1½ oz. Dubonnet Rouge

1½ oz. gin

1 dash Angostura bitters

Add ingredients into a shaker with ice. Stir for 30 seconds and strain into glass.

SCOFFLAW

This popular 1920s drink, created in Paris, has a name that speaks for itself. The term *scofflaw* derives from people who scoff at the law, an apt description for consumers of this Prohibition-era cocktail.

2 oz. bourbon or rye

1 oz. dry vermouth

¼ oz. fresh lemon juice

½ oz. grenadine

2 dashes bitters (orange)

Add ingredients to a cocktail shaker and fill with ice. Shake, and strain into a chilled cocktail glass.

BEE'S KNEES

This gin-forward cocktail is made with honey. As with a martini, the type of gin used will give completely different flavor profiles. Artisanal juniper-heavy gins offer a nice counterbalance to the sweetness of the honey.

2 oz. gin
¾ oz. honey
½ oz. lemon juice

Shake ingredients together in shaker with ice. Strain into chilled cocktail glass.

FRENCH 75

Created in 1915 in Paris, the French 75 has champagne as one its main ingredients. The most well-known recipe of this drink appeared in *The Savoy Cocktail Book* in 1930.This cocktail managed to stay popular through Prohibition and beyond.

¾ oz. gin
⅓ part lemon juice
Spoonful of powdered sugar
Champagne

Pour first three ingredients into glass filled with crushed ice and stir. Top with champagne.

GIN RICKEY

1½ oz. gin
1 lime, juiced
½ tsp. confectioners' sugar
Seltzer

Fill glass with ice and add gin, lime juice, and sugar. Stir. Add seltzer, and garnish with a lime wedge.

Whiskey

Whiskey ruled the bootlegging world in the northern United States, especially around the Great Lakes, where proximity to Canada and a bountiful supply of Canadian whiskey was just what enterprising booze sellers needed for a successful business. Bootleggers also brought in whiskey from the British Isles, the venture profitable enough for them to risk a trans-Atlantic voyage. Whiskey became not only an easy commodity to smuggle, but one that could be watered down and colored to maximize profits.

Detroit-based gangsters Joe Zerilli, Bill Tocco, and Pete Licavoli smuggled liquor over the Great Lakes, and were "engaged in the rum

Prohibition-era still operation in New York City discovered by the NYPD. Stills were located in industrial areas, abandoned warehouses, and even apartments. Photo credit: NYC Municipal Archives.

running activities in Detroit," according to the FBI. Tocco and Licavoli became top mob figures in Detroit and Cleveland, respectively, using the millions earned by smuggling whiskey to turn their crime families into two of the most influential during that time. Powerful Las Vegas mobster Moe Dalitz got his start as part of the infamous Purple Gang and oversaw the shipping of Canadian whiskey across the lakes as well, transporting the product throughout the Upper Midwest.

Whiskey was also distilled throughout regions of the United States. Still operations were a common site during, and well after, Prohibition in the Midwest and Appalachia. The widespread mob influence seen in the major cities was not as pronounced in rural areas. Here, control of the liquor rackets was a local affair. But crime organizations did exist from the backwoods of Kentucky and West Virginia down through the South, hotbeds of illegal distilleries. One example was the cracker mob of rural Florida, a loose-knit confederation of criminals that stayed outside the big metro areas and controlled liquor smuggling and production in addition to the usual rackets of gambling and prostitution.

WARD 8

The Ward 8 was created in Boston in 1898, at least according to one version of its origin story. Another version claims the drink was created in New York City. By the 1920s the Ward 8 was a popular cocktail especially suited to less-than-premium whiskeys as the other flavors could mask the taste of the substandard liquor.

2 oz. rye whiskey
¾ oz. lemon juice
¾ oz. simple syrup
Grenadine
Orange slice
Maraschino cherry

Pour first four ingredients into a cocktail shaker with ice. Shake well and strain into chilled cocktail glass. Garnish with orange slice and cherry.

Old Fashioned

The Old Fashioned remains a popular drink to this day. It survived Prohibition in part because it was easy to make. Also, the addition of sugar and some fruit could mask if a speakeasy was serving substandard or watered-down whiskey.

The Old Fashioned was believed to have first appeared in the late 1800s, at the Pendennis Club in Louisville, Kentucky. The club is, according to its website, "a gathering of friends, where decency, decorum, civility, good manners and the social graces are still very much in style." In other words, exactly the type of place where a traditional drink like the Old Fashioned would be conceived.

Robert Simonson, *New York Times* spirits writer, is a fan: "Though I drink more gin and whiskey than anything else, my favorite cocktail is an Old Fashioned because it's classic, simple, versatile, lets the spirit shine, and fits the ancient definition of a cocktail," Simonson said.

Over the years, there have been some changes and additions to the drink. Some bartenders, for example, add a splash of club soda on top. But while opinions on how best to make this drink may vary, at its heart the recipe is simple. It's a mixture of sweet, bitter, liquor, and water.

OLD FASHIONED

1 sugar cube
2 dashes Angostura bitters
1 splash water
2 oz. bourbon
Slice lemon peel
Slice orange
Cherry

Muddle the sugar cube, bitters, and water in an old-fashioned glass. Add the bourbon. Stir. Add ice. Twist the lemon peel over the glass and add. Drop in orange and cherry if desired. That's it. Uncomplicated and delicious.

With such a simple drink, it is essential to not cheap out on the main ingredient. For bourbons, I like Bulleit, Eagle Rare, and Jefferson's Reserve. Buffalo Trace is another good choice.

Moonshine

Known by many names—hooch, white whiskey—moonshine is typically distilled from corn. The "white lightning" is often associated with the backwoods of Appalachia or the Deep South, where citizens would set up still operations far from the prying eyes of law enforcement. Though moonshine had been made in the US since the 1800s, it wasn't until Prohibition that the aura around it and the associated bootlegging activity became part of American culture.

(During that era, trafficking in moonshine—for which being able to drive fast enough to evade the law was an occupational requirement—even gave rise to one of the most popular sports in the United States today: NASCAR.)

Even after Prohibition ended, moonshining continued to be a lucrative racket for backwoods

A varied cache of bootleg liquor seized during Prohibition. This particular batch was of a little higher quality than the usual spirits smuggled into the US. Photo credit: Christian Cipollini.

BLONDE MANHATTAN

This recipe combines the unique sweet strength of corn whiskey with the bitter orange flavor of Cointreau for a twist on the classic Manhattan.

1¾ oz. Hudson New York Moonshine Corn Whiskey
1 oz. Antica Sweet Vermouth
½ oz. Cointreau
3 dashes orange bitters
1 lemon twist

Stir the first four ingredients with ice and strain over fresh ice into rocks glass. Garnish with lemon twist.

gangsters. Crime syndicates like the Dixie Mafia and the Cracker Mob in Florida not only maintained still operations, but also transported bootleg liquor, especially popular in dry counties.

An early 1960s government report on "Crime Conditions in Dallas" stated, "Reliable informants advised that police pressure in both Texas and Miller County, Arkansas had about curtailed all moonshine operations." The report also noted that their law enforcement compatriots a few states over had a different situation, namely that "moonshiners in Pearl River County are the principal sources of moonshine whiskey in the Southern District of Mississippi."

Moonshine is now legal in most states. Just a decade ago, it wasn't. With this change moonshine has become a popular spirit. Though it's not as easy to mix into a cocktail as some other types of whiskey, there is a growing movement of mixologists who are using this truly American spirit in creative ways.

Post Prohibition

When Prohibition ended, the mob did not exit the liquor industry. Quite the contrary. Over the ensuing years, the mob invested large sums of money in retooling illegal bootlegging operations into legitimate breweries and distilleries. Other mobsters started liquor distributorships. And owning a bar or lounge became de rigeur for gangsters from all the major cities in the United States. Bars and lounges made excellent hangouts and places to conduct business. They were also ideal for laundering the proceeds from rackets such as illegal gambling or drugs.

"From a business perspective, many of the guys from the shadowy 'Seven Group/Big Seven' and others knew that buying into legitimate and established distilleries and breweries was a smart post-prohibition move," said Christian Cipollini, author of *Murder Inc.* "Now, of course, we are talking about mobsters, so legitimacy was far from where all the gangsters ventured and remained. Besides the legal endeavors of liquor and even gambling legitimately to some extent, many of the big guns also went wholeheartedly into another prohibited racket—narcotics. But booze was the catalyst in creating what we all know and recognize as the original gangsters."

One city where the mob infiltrated all aspects of the legitimate liquor industry was Tampa. From the earliest years of organized crime in the Cigar City, underworld figures owned restaurants and bars. By the time of Prohibition, Tampa was one of the largest ports of entry for illicit rum from Cuba and the Caribbean. The bars that were

Post-Prohibiton Brooklyn Beer Garden circa 1934 after a fight between gangsters Vito Gurino and Happy Maione. Gurino and Maione were both purported members of the mob hit squad Murder, Inc. Photo credit: Christian Cipollini.

nightclubs and casinos before Prohibition maintained their allure as speakeasies and bolita palaces. Bolita was a lottery-style game so popular in Tampa that everyone from gangsters to judges, cops, and politicians played.

When Prohibition ended the bars opened up as legal establishments. Some mobsters, like Salvatore "Red" Italiano, went into business for themselves. Italiano owned and operated a distributorship,

Anthony Distributors, which handled Miller products. His brother owned a bar in Ybor City, the Latin section of Tampa. Other mobsters joined suit, and by the 1950s most of the major organized crime figures in Tampa owned bars or were otherwise involved in the liquor industry. Mob boss Santo Trafficante Jr. was often heard to brag that he had the State Beverage Commissioner in his pocket and was able to guide liquor licenses to favored mob colleagues.

Bootleggers' warehouse with barrels stacked, waiting to be filled. Photo credit: Library of Congress.

MONKEY GLAND

This 1920s creation, devised at Harry's New York bar in Paris, took its name from a medical procedure for men with performance issues. Supposedly, the testicle of a monkey was implanted to help revive the men's libido. The procedure was developed by Russian surgeon Dr. Serge Voronoff, who practiced medicine in France.

The drink itself uses absinthe, the mysterious licorice-flavored liqueur banned for decades in the United States. It's now widely available and free of its legendary hallucinogenic properties (though many doubt it ever had them to begin with).

1½ oz. gin

1½ oz. orange juice

1 tsp. grenadine

1 tsp. absinthe

Pour ingredients into shaker with ice. Shake vigorously and strain into a chilled cocktail glass.

CHAPTER 3

Crime Novelists and Their Characters

There's something so romantically noir about quiet conversations in a dark, smoky bar—plots hatched, secrets revealed, confessions whispered.

LISA UNGER, AUTHOR

Readers show a never-ending fascination with plotlines ranging from straightforward murder mysteries to convoluted heists and scams. Crime fiction dates back at least to 1841, with the publication of Edgar Allan Poe's tale "The Murders in the Rue Morgue." Starting in the late 1800s, the genre got a big boost from Sir Arthur Conan Doyle's Sherlock Holmes books. By the 1920s and '30s, pulp magazines were bringing the hardboiled detective to readers hungry for escapist stories. The genre branched out into a variety of subcategories, including detective fiction, pulp, and hardboiled stories.

Crime fiction is perhaps the most cocktail-centric of all literary genres, and for good reason.

"There's something so romantically noir about quiet conversations in a dark, smoky bar—plots hatched, secrets revealed, confessions whispered," said bestselling mystery author Lisa Unger. "There's something edgy, too, about a place where people gather just to drink. It's a place where any group of shady characters might get together to discuss their nefarious intentions. And then, of course, alcohol is a kind of truth serum, isn't it?"

Unger offered a further explanation for this marriage of literature and alcohol. "Maybe the answer is simply that so many writers, the shadiest characters of all, are drinkers. You'll never go to a writers' conference and not spend a lot of time at the bar, and that goes double for a mystery writers' conference. So perhaps it's a write-what-you-know kind of a thing."

Raymond Chandler

Raymond Chandler was one of the founding fathers of the literary genre known as hardboiled, in which the action is most often seen through the eyes of a cynical, steely private eye. Many of the stories were published in literary magazines dedicated to the genre, others in the pulp magazines of the 1930s and '40s. Hardboiled crime fiction also bled into comic books.

Chandler's most famous character was Philip Marlowe. Though popular first in print, the private investigator became a cultural touchstone on screen, portrayed memorably by actors as diverse as Humphrey Bogart, Powers Boothe, Elliott Gould, and Robert Mitchum. Marlowe was as rough and rugged as any literary detective, no stranger to the pitfalls of femme fatales and clients who weren't always as truthful as they should be. And Marlowe knew his way around drinks, both as an imbiber and as one who used booze to his advantage.

Author Raymond Chandler, one of the most influential novelists and screenwriters in crime fiction history. His hardboiled writing became the template for the genre in the 1940s. Photo credit: author collection.

Marlowe always kept an office bottle. You know—the one sitting in the drawer devoid of anything but a bottle of whiskey—or in Marlowe's case, Old Forester bourbon. "I reached down and put the bottle of Old Forester on the desk. It was about a third full," Marlowe says in the novel *The Little Sister*. He shifts from narrating the action to rambling to himself. "Now who gives you that pal? That's green-label stuff. Out of your class entirely. Must have been a client. I had a client once."

Toby Widdicome's book *A Reader's Guide to Raymond Chandler* presents a comprehensive list of the drinks featured in the author's work: "In 'Finger Man' there's Bacardi, and in 'Big City Blues' Bacardi and grenadine. In *The High Window*, there's Four Roses Whiskey. In 'Wrong Pigeon' there are double Gibsons." The list also includes Old Grand-Dad whiskey and Brooklyn Scotch.

Chandler enjoyed drinking, in fact more than he should. Though at times he managed to keep himself clean, he was an alcoholic. While writing the script for the Paramount movie *The Blue Dahlia*, he proposed to the studio that he stay at home, where "he'd drink steadily, eat no solid food and subsist on glucose injections from his doctor." Over the course of eight days, Chandler belted out the script, consuming copious amounts of whiskey. He did good work, but it took him a month to recover.

The Gimlet

While the Gimlet has many variations, at its base it is a showcase for gin mixed with a few other ingredients.

In Chandler's noir classic *The Long Goodbye*, English ex-pat and enthusiastic drinker Terry Lennox tells Philip Marlowe that "A real gimlet is half gin and half Rose's Lime Juice and nothing else. It beats martinis hollow."

Marlowe then takes his first look. "The bartender set the drink in front of me. With the lime juice it has a sort of pale greenish yellowish misty look. I tasted it. It was both sweet and sharp at the same time. The woman in black watched me. Then she lifted her own glass towards me. We both drank. Then I knew hers was the same drink."

This literary gimlet has become the de facto recipe for gimlets in bars across the US. It's a simple recipe, perfect for experimenting on, riffing with, and deconstructing. Replacing Rose's with fresh lime juice and St-Germain Elderflower liqueur is a start. Or one could substitute vodka for gin.

The way Lennox describes a gimlet is perhaps a little too sweet for most people. I prefer a different mix.

Dashiell Hammett

An American author best known for hardboiled crime novels, Dashiell Hammett penned *The*

Rose's Lime Juice made its debut in 1867. It combines lime juice with sweeteners and coloring. It was introduced to America in 1901.

GIMLET

2 oz. gin
¾ oz. Rose's Lime Juice
Add to cocktail shaker with ice. Shake vigorously for 30 seconds. Strain into cocktail glass.

STINGER

Another favorite cocktail of Chandler's was the Stinger, a minty libation that dates back to the 1890s. It has an uncomplicated recipe but a complex taste. It shows up in a few film noirs as well, including Chandler's 1947 *The Big Clock*.

2 oz. cognac
1 oz. white crème de menthe
Mix both ingredients in a shaker with ice. Shake vigorously and strain into a glass with ice.

Maltese Falcon, which was adapted into one of the greatest Hollywood noirs of all time. Published in 1931, *Falcon* centers on private detective Sam Spade. Spade is not always a likable guy. He can be shifty and distant. He's a womanizer. But he is loyal. And he does imbibe. In *The Maltese Falcon*, Spade drinks a pre-mixed Manhattan from a paper cup, in keeping with his blue-collar, tough-guy persona. When he tips back a wine glass, it's filled with Bacardi rum.

Movie poster for the movie adaptation of Dashiel Hammett's *The Thin Man* (1934). This booze-fueled comedic noir was the first of six *Thin Man* movies starring William Powell and Myrna Loy. Photo credit: author collection.

With *The Glass Key*, published in 1931, Hammett departs from his detective novels, instead focusing on a racketeer. Here, too, the drinks flow. The main character in *The Glass Key* is a scotch drinker who also orders the occasional Manhattan.

Hammett himself was a heavy drinker. By the end of his life, it is fair to say, he was a serious alcoholic. He wrote his favorite drinks into his books. But unlike the author, his characters indulged all they wanted without suffering consequences. No one more so than Hammett's semi-autobiographical character, Nick Charles.

Nick and Nora Charles

Nora: "All I want is a hot bath."

Nick: "I will take a hot bath and a cold drink."

The husband-and-wife detective team of Nick and Nora Charles, protagonists of the *Thin Man* series of books and movies, are among Hammett's most popular creations. Many sources claim that Hammett based Nick Charles loosely on his own life (Hammett spent time as a Pinkerton detective). Though not dark noir, the *Thin Man* series did often feature murder, gangsters, and lots of shadows. But any sense of menace was offset by the tireless banter between Nick and Nora, as well as their exuberant drinking.

"Of course, the most booze-fueled book of all time is Hammett's *The Thin Man*. You can get a contact high just reading the damn thing," said neo-noir revivalist Eddie Muller. "Nobody ever made getting loaded look more glamorous."

A number of cocktails appear in the books and movie series. Most are variations on the martini, a popular drink of the time and one that reflected the insouciantly elegant way that Nick and Nora partook of their libations.

NICK AND NORA DRY MARTINI

1½ oz. dry gin
½ oz. dry vermouth
Olive without pimento
Stir with ice, strain into martini glass.

THE BRONX COCKTAIL

1½ oz. gin
½ oz. sweet vermouth
½ oz. dry vermouth
1 oz. orange juice
Combine all ingredients into a cocktail shaker with ice. Shake vigorously and strain into a cocktail glass with orange peel for garnish.

KNICKERBOCKER

1½ oz. gin
Dash of sweet vermouth
Dash of dry vermouth
Add ingredients to mixing glass with ice. Stir and strain into chilled martini glass.

James M. Cain

James M. Cain helped define the hardboiled crime genre not only for readers but for moviegoers. Three of his books were adapted into classic noir films, *Double Indemnity* (1944), *Mildred Pierce* (1941, 2011), and *The Postman Always Rings Twice* (1946, 1981). Cain passed away in 1977, but left behind a manuscript that was discovered and published in 2012 under the title *The Cocktail Waitress*.

Booze shows up throughout Cain's books, especially during scenes involving illicit lovers. Consider *The Postman Always Rings Twice*, narrated by Frank Chambers, who falls for Cora, a classic femme fatale. Turns out Cora is married to a diner operator, Nick (called "the Greek"), but wants out. Cora seduces Frank into helping her kill Nick so she can get the diner.

> I went to my room and got the liquor. It was a quart of Bourbon, three quarters full. I went down, got some Coca Cola glasses, and ice cubes, and White Rock, and came back upstairs. She had taken her hat off and her hair down. I fixed two drinks. They had some White Rock in them, and a couple pieces of ice, but the rest was out of the bottle.

I pushed her over to the bed. She held on to her glass and some of it spilled. "The hell with it. Plenty more where that came from."

. . . I began slipping off her blouse.

The White Rock described above is the sparkling mineral water now part of White Rock Beverages Company, which produces a variety of mixers. In the 1930s and '40s, White Rock sparkling water was often advertised as the perfect accompaniment to bourbon and rye.

Double Indemnity, originally printed as a magazine piece, became one of Cain's most famous works, thanks to the film adaptation directed by Billy Wilder, with a screenplay co-written by Raymond Chandler.

The movie is famous for its banter between insurance salesman Walter Neff (played by Fred MacMurray) and Phyllis Dietrichson (Barbara Stanwyck) as they encircle each other in attraction and deception. This scene sets the stage for their plot to off Phyllis's husband in a way that will trigger the double indemnity clause on his insurance, giving Phyllis a double pay-out.

NEFF: I'm crazy about you baby.

PHYLLIS: I'm crazy about you, Walter.

NEFF: That perfume on your hair. What's the name of it?

THE POSTMAN COCKTAIL

Not a direct call-out to Cain's novel, this cocktail has a definite beach feel to it, worlds away from the scheming femme fatales and morally ambiguous characters that populate James Cain's literary universe.

2 oz. vodka
1 oz. 151-proof rum
2 oz. orange juice
1 oz. cranberry juice
½ oz. grenadine

Add all ingredients to a cocktail shaker with ice. Shake vigorously. Strain into glass.

PHYLLIS: Something French, I bought it down at Ensenada.

NEFF: We ought to have some of that pink wine to go with it. The kind that bubbles. But all I have is bourbon.

PHYLLIS: Bourbon is fine, Walter.

NEFF: Soda?

PHYLLIS: Plain water please.

NEFF: Get a couple of glasses will ya? You know about six months ago a guy slipped on the soap in his bathtub and knocked himself cold and drowned. Only he had accident insurance. So they had an autopsy and she didn't get away with it.

PHYLLIS: Who didn't?

NEFF: His wife. And there was another case where a guy was found shot and his wife said he was cleaning a gun and stomach got in the way. All she collected was a three-to-ten stretch in Tehachapi.

PHYLLIS: Perhaps it was worth it to her.

Ross Macdonald

Ross Macdonald (the pseudonym of Kenneth Millar) was a highly regarded hardboiled noir writer. Almost all of his novels and stories featured PI Lew Archer. Macdonald's creation is a little less rough than Marlowe or Spade, but possesses the same sense of world weariness.

Though Lew Archer doesn't drink as heavily as many noir PIs, he does enjoy some of the usual suspects in the liquor cabinet. In 1959's *The Galton Case,* he drinks gin and tonics and Gibsons. In 1961's *The Wicherly Woman,* he tries Goldwater (an herbal liqueur), but says, "the drink is a little too sweet for me. I'm going to switch to bourbon." He tries bourbon again in a number of novels, including *The Drowning Pool*. And in 1954's *Find a Victim,* Archer discovers murder amidst a hijacked shipment of $70,000 worth of bourbon.

Mickey Spillane

A literary descendent of Chandler and Hammett, Mickey Spillane (not to be confused with the mobster of the same name) was one of the most successful authors in the genre. His best-known creation, private investigator Mike Hammer, appeared in over twenty books, some of which were finished after Spillane's death in 2006, and in popular TV and movie adaptations. Hammer differed from Sam Spade and Philip Marlowe. He was rougher around the edges and more prone to violence, often vividly described in the novels. Hammer smoked, drank, and slept with a lot of women.

His drink of choice was as no-frills as you'd expect. Spillane famously said, "Mike Hammer drinks beer instead of cognac because I can't spell cognac."

Spillane was not a big drinker, preferring only the occasional beer. One beer that he will forever be associated with is Miller Lite. Spillane was the pitchman for the brand through the 1970s, uttering the line, "All you ever wanted from a beer, and less." Many of the commercials had a noir theme, with Spillane decked out in a trench coat and hat, echoing Mike Hammer.

Today's crime novelists carry on the examples set by Chandler, Hammett, and Spillane in having their characters reflect their real-world tastes for booze.

Bestselling author Dennis Lehane is one of the most successful of modern crime writers. A number of his books, inlcuding *Gone Baby Gone* and *Mystic River* have been made into movies. Photo credit: Ashleigh-Faye Beland.

Dennis Lehane

Boston-bred author Dennis Lehane has written some of the most successful mystery books of the last decade. From *Mystic River* to *Shutter Island* to *Gone, Baby Gone*, his novels exude the sense of a modern noir. Lehane has also written for television crime dramas including *The Wire* and *Boardwalk Empire*.

"I'm mostly a beer guy, Beck's, which is not surprisingly what most of my characters drink because it's what all guys out of the neighborhoods drink in Boston. Every now and then I'll have a vodka-n-tonic or a gin-n-tonic and even more rarely I might have a scotch or an Irish whiskey neat (Middleton, usually), but at the end of the day, you can take the boy out of Dorchester but you can't take Dorchester out of the boy."

Lisa Unger

A New York Times bestselling author of thirteen suspense and mystery novels, Lisa Unger has more than professional skills in common with her most famous character, true crime writer Lydia Strong, who keeps chilled Ketel One Vodka on hand.

"There's always a bottle of vodka in my freezer," Unger said. "At the moment it's a bottle of Reyka, which we brought back with us from a recent trip to Iceland. It's one of the best vodkas I've ever had—very smooth, best served straight up and ice cold. I am a vodka girl—Grey Goose, Ketel One, or Absolut, usually. I don't drink much else. There's nothing that tastes as light and clean—as far as liquor goes, anyway. There might be the occasional Margarita or Mojito, but my go-to drink is either a Cosmopolitan or, more often, Grey Goose and soda."

Walter Mosley

In books centering on LA private investigator Easy Rawlins, Walter Mosley portrays Los Angeles' jazz club past with a strong noir undercurrent. And though Mosley does not drink, in his 2002 novel *Black Betty*, Rawlins has this eloquent ode to whiskey:

MIMOSA

The mimosa is basically a variation of a classic champagne cocktail, though it's associated more with late morning brunches than cocktail lounges.

2½ oz. orange juice
2½ oz. champagne

Chill a champagne flute. Add cold orange juice and chilled champagne. Stir gently to mix.

"Elder Darrow, the protagonist of my mystery novel Solo Act, is the owner and chief bartender at the Esposito in Boston's South End. He drinks scotch, single-malt, but he understands that mixed drinks, the more elaborate the better, are his moneymakers. His particular bugaboo is the pousse-cafe, an elaborately constructed cocktail in which various fruit juices,liquors, and liqueurs are carefully poured on top of each other to create a series of different-colored layers. It's a drink for looking at, not swallowing, and he can't imagine how horrible they must taste."

(Dick Cass)

"There are few things as beautiful as a glass bottle filled with deep amber whiskey. Liquor shines when the light hits it, reminiscent of precious things like jewels and gold. But whiskey is better than some lifeless bracelet or coronet. Whiskey is a living thing capable of any emotion that you are. It's love and deep laughter and brotherhood of the type that bonds nations together. Whiskey is your friend when nobody else comes around. And whiskey is solace that holds you tighter than most lovers can."

Eddie Muller

Eddie "Czar of Noir" Muller earned his nickname writing novels, biographies, movie histories, plays, short stories, and films. He has twice been named a San Francisco Literary Laureate. As founder of the Film Noir Foundation, he's led the effort to save numerous at-risk examples of the form, including *The Prowler*, *Cry Danger*, *Try and Get Me!*, *Too Late for Tears*, and *Woman on the Run*.

His taste in cocktails runs pretty much as you might expect from someone with such respect for tradition. "I tend to stick with the classics—martini, Manhattan, the occasional Negroni and an Old Fashioned. It really depends on the weather and the setting, doesn't it? Whether you're drinking for camaraderie or solitude, before dinner, after dinner, or in the middle of a lazy afternoon."

Dick Cass

Dick Cass lives, writes, drinks, and fishes in Cape Elizabeth, Maine. He's as fond of a shot of good scotch as the next soul, but if you restricted him to one libation, it would be wine: Pinot Noir from California's Russian River Valley or Oregon Pinot Gris. He is the author of *Gleam of Bone*, a book of short stories, and *Solo Act*, a jazz mystery.

Dick Cass, author of the jazz-themed mystery *Solo Act*. Photo credit: Dick Cass.

"I tend to be a seasonal cocktail drinker, with favorites for different seasons and situations. It's partly a function of a short attention span. Spring drinking is usually light, a habanero Bloody Mary or a Mimosa on a Sunday morning, maybe a Salty Dog for variety and the extra Vitamin C after a long dark winter.

"The only summer cocktail for me, Memorial Day to Labor Day, is the classic gin and tonic, preferably made with a locally made gin like Chesuncook or Ingenium. Late summer, when the mint is best, I'll down a Mojito or two.

BLOODY MARY

The ultimate morning drink, beloved by many for its hangover curative powers. Possibly the most ordered drink in airport bars before the first flight of the day. However, never drink three with a cigar, before 10 a.m., in Las Vegas, during March Madness. Just don't.

This is a version of the classic Bloody Mary recipe, from Liquor.com.

Lemon wedge
Lime wedge
1 pinch celery salt
2 oz. vodka
4 oz. tomato juice
2 dashes Tabasco sauce
2 tbsp. horseradish
2 dashes horseradish
1 pinch black pepper

Pour celery salt onto a small plate. Rub the lemon or lime wedge along the lip of a pint glass. Roll the outer edge of the glass in celery salt until fully coated. Fill with ice and set aside.

Squeeze the lemon and lime wedges into a shaker and drop them in. Add the remaining ingredients and fill with ice. Shake gently and strain into the glass. Garnish with a celery stalk and a lime wedge.

"Fall and winter are the darker months for the darker liquors: bourbon sours or a dram of Caol Ila or Macallan 18 with a drop of water. And year-round, any time: fresh-poured Guinness."

C. Michele Dorsey

C. "Michele" Dorsey is the author of mysteries including *No Virgin Island*, set in her preferred getaway destination, St. John, USVI. In fiction and in real life, she matches her drinks to her setting.

"My favorite summer/island cocktail is a lemon drop made with Crop Organic Meyer Lemon Vodka," Dorsey said. "In winter, I switch to a Tanqueray martini, straight up, no vermouth, with olives marinated in lemon and a little minced garlic.

"The main character in my book *No Virgin Island* is meteorologist turned villa agent Sabrina Salter. Life on sunny St. John is a welcome escape from Boston—until her sexiest guest turns up murdered, and since she's the last person who saw him alive (and naked), she's the prime suspect. Sabrina turns to a former lawyer, now waterfront bar owner, for legal advice and a steady supply of Stoli Citron on the rocks doused with plenty of fresh lemon juice to get her through."

> "Drinking was a way of life on an island, probably because almost everyone here had come to escape from somewhere, someone, or something. Sometimes all three. It was okay to drink enough to be numb, but not enough to duplicate the same kind of problems you were trying to leave behind."
>
> No Virgin Island

Waterfront bars figure prominently in Dorsey's work. She has strong opinions on what makes a great beach bar: You must be able to sit with your feet in the sand, look out at the water, and sip your favorite drink. Talking should be optional.

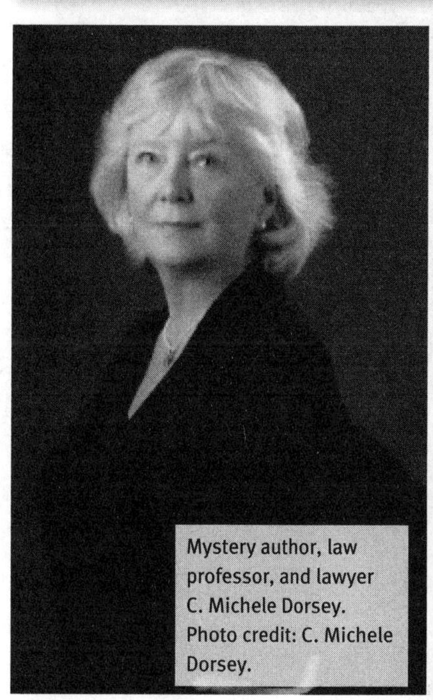

Mystery author, law professor, and lawyer C. Michele Dorsey. Photo credit: C. Michele Dorsey.

James Crumley

Thoroughly rooted in modern noir, James Crumley's mysteries (including *The Last Good Kiss* and *The Wrong Case*) are packed full of bars, beer, and seedy characters.

In Crumley's 1975 novel, *The Wrong Case*, private investigator Milo Milodragovitch offers this soliloquy

Nicholas Denmon chronicles the fictional workings of upstate New York mobsters in his books. Photo credit: Nicholas Denmon.

on imbibing: "Son, never trust a man who doesn't drink because he's probably a self-righteous sort, a man who thinks he knows right from wrong all the time. Some of them are good men, but in the name of goodness, they cause most of the suffering in the world. They're the judges, the meddlers. And, son, never trust a man who drinks but refuses to get drunk. They're usually afraid of something deep down inside, either that they're a coward or a fool or mean and violent. You can't trust a man who's afraid of himself. But sometimes, son, you can trust a man who occasionally kneels before a toilet. The chances are that he is learning something about humility and his natural human foolishness, about how to survive himself. It's damned hard for a man to take himself too seriously when he's heaving his guts into a dirty toilet bowl."

After his death in 2008, Crumley received an honor that would surely have pleased both him and Milo. His favorite steakhouse—The Depot in Missoula, Minnesota—named a bar stool in his memory.

Laura Lippman

Baltimore reporter-turned-bestselling-author Laura Lippman's most popular recurring character is Baltimore reporter-turned-private eye Tess Monaghan. Tess enjoys wine. So does Lippman.

"I love Chardonnay. I love very good Chardonnay. And I love those big fat plummy red wines that Robert Parker loves," Lippman said. "But if I regret anything, it's that I started drinking better wine, which ruined cheap Chardonnay for me."

SALTY DOG

The Salty Dog is basically a Greyhound with salt on the glass rim.

Kosher or coarse sea salt
1½ oz. dry gin (or vodka)
3½ oz. grapefruit juice

Pour salt in a small dish. Wet the edge of a highball glass and coat the edge with the salt. Add ice to the glass. Add the gin and grapefruit juice. Stir.

Nicholas Denmon

Nicholas Denmon is the author of a trilogy of Mafia novels, *For Nothing, Buffalo Soldiers,* and *Ashes to Ashes,* all set in upstate New York. When drinking, Denmon keeps it simple.

"I may be a bit old fashioned, but if I'm not having a beer, I really just prefer a scotch and a splash of water. When I'm at a bar, I usually just grab a Johnny Walker Black. At home, however, I have a little known favorite, Sheildaig Speyside Single Malt. They hold it in an old oak cast for eighteen years and the flavor has a hint of spice, smoke, and oak. I absolutely love it. When I write, I like to have a solitary drink, so this is my go-to drink of choice during the week."

George Pelecanos

One of the top modern noir writers, George Pelecanos takes arguably the most cutthroat city in America—Washington, DC—and exposes its lawless underbelly, eschewing the usual dirty politics plots of so many DC-centered novels. He also writes for the acclaimed crime series *The Wire*. His novels feature a variety of drinks, from the cognac with a side glass of water in *Shoedog* to the martinis in *Down by The River Where the Dead Men Go*.

Pelecanos often uses cocktails to set the scene and reveal character traits. In his 2001 book *Right as Rain*, Pelecanos evocatively describes the way meth-dealer Ray Boone makes a cocktail. "Ray grabbed the black-labeled bottle and a tumbler, filled the glass with ice from the chest behind the sink, and free-poured sour mash whiskey halfway to the lip. He filled the rest of the glass with Coke and stirred the cocktail with a dirty finger."

Florida Noir

Florida is a state unlike any other. Just listen to the evening news and you're guaranteed to hear that some bizarre, unbelievable thing happened in Florida. More than any other place in America, it's a fascinating mix of old-time residents, retirees, immigrants, newly arrived second-chancers, and anyone looking to find a place in paradise. It's the only US state where you have to drive north to get into the Deep South. It's Spanish moss and live oaks, scrub pines and palm trees, white sand and sandy soil.

But that's only half the picture. Florida has always been home to a noxious mix of transients, schemers, gangsters, crooked politicians, con men, and some of the strangest crimes imaginable. It's where the Cocaine Cowboys brought a mythos to drug smuggling, the cracker mob ran gambling and moonshining well into the late twentieth century in the rural backwoods, and where American mobsters mixed with gangsters from Cuba, Russia, Israel, and all of Central and South America. Florida is literally the end of the road in America.

With the flat-out weirdness of the state, a unique genre of crime fiction has developed over the decades. Collectively known as Florida Noir, it showcases the state's seedier side, usually with touches of humor and generous helpings of cocktails, beach bars, and rum. One of the most popular scribes in this genre is Carl Hiaasen, whose witty observations of the Sunshine State have become part of the very lore of Florida. There are also Randy Wayne White, Tim Dorsey, Edna Buchanan, Elmore Leonard, John D. MacDonald, and so many other talented writers who call Florida both their home and their muse.

J. David Gonzalez, in a 2013 piece for *Salon*, takes the history of Florida Noir back to A.C. Guner's 1896 novel *Don Balascao of Key West*. The thread of criminality ran through Florida fiction throughout the early twentieth century, but really exploded in the 1960s, around the time traditional noir started falling out of favor.

Author Bob Morris offered an explanation for why Florida Noir has become such a popular sub-genre of crime fiction: "As plenty of people before me have observed: You can't make up the stuff that happens here. Sooner or later all the loose nuts roll this way. We've long since out-weirded California.

"I set my books in Florida and the Caribbean—Baja Florida, as I refer to it—because the islands can out-weird Florida. The characters are even more bent and twisted, the money more funny, the governments and law enforcement even more corrupt, and it is perfectly acceptable to have beer for breakfast, especially if it is Guinness Export Special."

Bob Morris

Drinks flow in Morris's Zack Chasteen series of mysteries (*Bahamarama, Jamaica Me Dead, Bermuda Schwartz, Baja Florida*).

"Zack Chasteen, the main guy in my novels, is a rum lover extraordinaire. He prefers it neat, but won't turn it down with a bit of lime. And he prefers it most any time of day. He is also an enthusiastic eater."

Morris tried to slip instructions for some of his character's favorite dishes and drinks into his first novel *Bahamarama*. "It had some recipes for cocktails and for things like conch fritters and Cuban bread. It was part of the narrative and I thought it fit nicely. But my editor didn't think such things belonged in a so-called 'crime' novel so I got rid of them. Fucking editors. . . ."

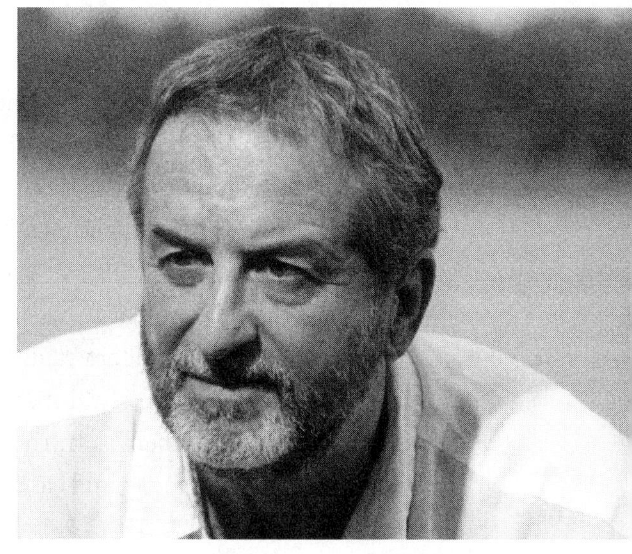

Florida Noir author, and rum enthusiast, Bob Morris. Photo credit: Bob Morris.

Morris himself enjoys a range of cocktails. "I love all the variations on a theme of Negroni and Boulevardier. I typically substitute Aperol for the Campari and add a splash of Hella Citrus Bitters. That said, nothing can beat a great gin and tonic, especially when the tonic is small batch and you add a floater of Fernet on top."

Bob's Perfect Rum Drink (this time, presented without editorial interference):

> I follow the age-old island recipe: One of sour, two of sweet, three of strong, four of weak. Essentially, that translates to a hand-stirred daiquiri, ideally with Flor de Cana or Mount Gay or Barbancourt Nine-Year. Then a splash of bitters to give it backbone and gumption.

Kate Flora

Award-winning writer Kate Flora is the author of fourteen books, most recently the true crime story *Death Dealer* and the novel *And Grant You Peace*. Kate's fiction includes the Thea Kozak mysteries and the Joe Burgess police series.

Flora's plots sometimes hinge on alcohol. In a cooperative work, *Beat, Flay, Love*, "One of the characters, a famous TV chef, is killed by the very signature cocktail she's designed for their Valentine cooking show," Flora said. "Here's a description of the Berry Drop: For the cocktail, she'd made a huckleberry syrup, and there would be glistening berries in the glass, and a special lemon liqueur and Grey Goose vodka and candied ginger. Poured carefully, so the layers didn't mix."

What the chef didn't count on was the poison slipped into her carefully crafted drink.

Cocktails also play a dark role in Flora's novella *Girls' Night Out*, about a woman's book group taking revenge on the man who drugged a drink and date-raped their friend. "When one of the women hooks up with this serial rapist at a bar, and he dumps a suspicious powder into her Cosmo, she switches drinks and he ends up drugging himself, with unfortunate consequences for the fellow."

Off the page, Flora prefers her cocktails considerably more benign. Her favorite? "A toss-up between a gin martini with two olives and a twist, and a Manhattan, heavy on the vermouth, with three cherries."

Brett Halliday

Brett Halliday was the pen name of writer David Dresser. Though he lived most of his life in California, the author's most famous creation was Michael Shayne, a Miami-based PI. Shayne made his debut in the 1939 novel *Dividend on Death*. The red-haired investigator appeared in over fifty Halliday novels (in addition to many more that Dresser contracted out to other authors). Halliday's novels were hardboiled detective fiction, and Shayne's popularity as a character was rivaled only by Marlowe and Spade in the pantheon of great literary PIs.

While many PIs enjoyed the harder edge of rye or scotch, Shayne's libation of choice was cognac. His love of the spirit peaked in the 1944 short novel *A Taste for Cognac*. The plot revolves around stolen cognac and is full of vivid descriptions of drinking:

> He soon came back from the kitchen with two four-ounce wine glasses and two tumblers filled with ice water. He walked

past her, arranged the four glasses in a row on the table, and filled the wine glasses to the brim with cognac. . . .

Shayne sighed when he drained the last drop from his glass of Monnet. He frowned at the portion remaining in Myrna's glass. "Don't you appreciate good liquor?" She smiled and told him: "It's so good I'm making it last."

CHAPTER 4

Mob Authors

When it comes to the relationship between drinking and writing, I subscribe to the 'method drinking' technique, which is like method acting, except with alcohol.

T.J. ENGLISH, AUTHOR

In 2004 I published my first book, a look inside the Tampa Mob, *Cigar City Mafia*, joining a tradition of true crime writing that stretches back to the early twentieth century. Edmund Lester Pearson's 1924 title, *Studies in Murder*, detailing five infamous homicides, is considered one of the first true crime books.

Since then, the genre has evolved in a number of ways. In the 1960s, while Truman Capote's *In Cold Blood* introduced the concept of a high-end true crime account that used novelistic techniques, more sensationalistic authors were discovering the money to be made turning stories of killers and con men into hastily written pulp paperbacks. Today, true crime is dominated by serial killers and tawdry tabloid sagas (e.g. JonBenet Ramsey). But, like most of the authors featured in this chapter, many readers are still drawn to stories of organized crime.

Gangster books began to appear on shelves in the mid-1950s, around the time that the nation was becoming aware of a shadowy nationwide syndicate purported to control all of America's crime (which, of course, the mob never did). The mob came to television in the early 1950s. Tennessee Senator Estes Kefauver led a traveling congressional investigative team across the country, holding hearings about organized crime and political corruption. The televised Kefauver hearings, followed by the 1957 police raid on a Mafia conclave in Apalachin, piqued public interest in the mob. Some of the earliest gangster books were part sensationalism, part urban myth. But by the 1960s authors like Hank Messick, Ed Reid, Peter Maas, and Gay Talese brought weight and an investigative reporter's eye to the subject and the genre really took off with titles like Maas's *The Valachi Papers*, Messick's *The Silent Syndicate*, and Talese's *Honor Thy Father*.

In 1986, Nicholas Pileggi's *Wiseguy* (which became the basis of the movie *Goodfellas*) opened the floodgates to mobster memoirs. Turncoat gangsters fresh off the stand testifying against their former cohorts began shopping around for literary agents and deals with top publishers.

Like every genre, gangster books ebb and flow in popularity. But since the late 1990s there has been an upswing in the genre not only from ex-gangsters looking to write their memoirs (Sammy Gravano, Phil Leonetti), but from historians and academics who have taken the study of organized crime out of pop culture and applied more rigorous standards of research and analysis.

T.J. English

T.J. English's mob books, including *Paddywhacked* and *Havana Nocturne*, are some of the best organized crime histories ever written. The former is an overview of the rise and fall of Irish gangsters, the latter a look at how the mob controlled Havana in the pre-Castro era.

But there is one book that, to me, redefined true crime writing. It is not only the most powerful work I've ever read about the mob, but without a doubt my all-time favorite nonfiction book across all genres. That book is English's *The Westies*, a gritty, noirish tale of Irish gangsters in New York's Hell's Kitchen. The book focuses mainly on the group's rise and fall, including its partnership with the Gambino crime family and ultimate takedown by law enforcement. *The*

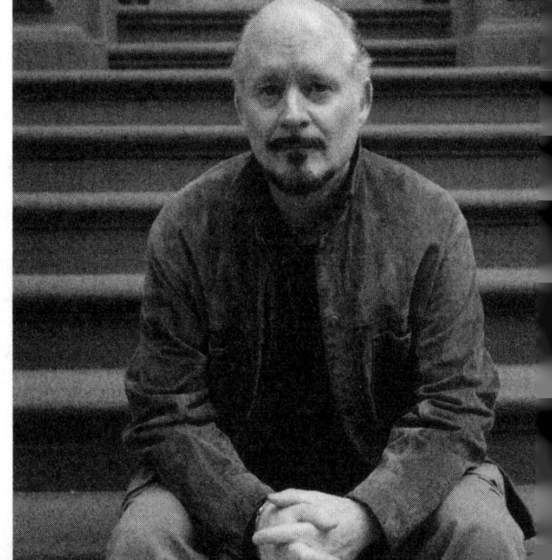

Author T.J. English has written extensively on organized crime, from Mexican cartels to the history of Irish mobsters in the United States. He is also one of the biggest influences on my writing. Photo credit: T.J. English.

Westies masterfully evokes a sense of time and place, the West Side of Manhattan in the 1970s and early '80s. It also captures the culture of the group, right down to its members' preferred spirit. The Westies drank Jameson's Irish Whiskey. So, for a while, did English:

"When it comes to the relationship between drinking and writing, I subscribe to the 'method drinking' technique, which is like method acting, except with alcohol," he said. "Has to do with using drinking as a way of getting into character. In other words, if you'd asked me what my favorite drink was when I was researching and writing *The Westies*, I would have said Jameson on the rocks. When writing *Havana Nocturne*, it was a mojito mulatta [a mojito with dark rum instead of silver]. Lately I've been doing research and writing on the narco war in Mexico, so it's nothing but tequila, preferably a good sipping tequila, like Don Julia añejo."

Mojito Mulatta

The key to making a quality mojito is obvious—use good rum and fresh mint leaves. No pre-bottled mixer will ever let you achieve the floral excellence of a well-muddled mojito. Perfect for a hot summer day, or sweltering night in the tropics, this drink is equally at home in a tropical noir tale or a tiki lounge.

There are a few variations on the standard mojito recipe, and an ongoing argument over how much club soda, if any, to include. This

DARK MOJITO

4–6 mint leaves
Lime juice (½ lime)
1 tsp. brown sugar
2 oz. dark rum
Club soda
Ice

Muddle the mint, lime juice, and brown sugar at the bottom of a tall glass. Add rum and ice. Stir with cocktail spoon or swizzle stick. Top off with club soda.

MOJITO

8–10 mint leaves
2 tbsp. simple syrup
½ lime
1½ oz. light rum
Club soda

Muddle all but one of the mint leaves with the simple syrup and lime. Add in ice and rum. Stir well. Top off with some club soda and garnish with remaining mint leaf.

dark rum mojito recipe is simple and refreshing. A number of affordable dark rums are good for mixing. Pyrat and Siesta Key (made in Florida) are two of my favorites. Keep the expensive stuff for sipping.

Jameson Irish Mule

This recipe from Jameson's is a take on the Moscow Mule, a classic cocktail that has enjoyed a resurgence in recent years.

The Moscow Mule was invented around 1941 by John Martin, a US representative for Smirnoff vodka. Though hard to imagine now,

MOSCOW MULE

You can find copper mugs online and in some housewares stores. Even if you don't have a copper mug, you can still make a Moscow Mule, though some purists would scoff at the notion. There are a variety of ginger beer brands available, including Gosling's, Fever Tree, Reed's, and Barritts.

2 oz. vodka
4–6 oz. ginger beer
1 tbsp. lime juice

Add ingredients in a copper mug with ice. Stir. Garnish with mint.

JAMESON MULE

The Jameson version replaces the vodka with its venerable Irish whiskey, and adds in some bitters for a nice contrast.

1½ oz. Jameson
Ginger beer
Bitters
Lime wedge

Fill glass or mug with ice. Add in Jameson shot. Pour in ginger beer to top, add 2–3 dashes of bitters, then stir. Squeeze the lime wedge and drop into Mule.

at that time vodka was not as ubiquitous in bars as it is today. Martin saw an opportunity to popularize vodka when he teamed with his friend John Morgan, who owned the Cock N' Bull on Sunset Boulevard in Hollywood.

Martin and Morgan combined the Cock N' Bull's homemade ginger beer with vodka, serving the concoction in a copper mug. Though the drink fell out of favor for a couple of decades, it has returned to drink menus across the country, resurrected as a hipster favorite.

The Westie

This drink was created by Fredo Ceraso, author, editor, and mixologist in New York City. "I was working on a St. Patrick's Day cocktail that was uniquely NYC," he said. "I thought of *The Westies*, T.J. English's book, and what they would drink. Then I extrapolated from there and focused on [Mickey] Spillane, the last old school Irish boss of Hell's Kitchen."

Unlike cocktail recipes that call for generic spirits, this one insists on brand-specific ingredients. It starts with Redbreast 12-year-old Single Pot Still Irish Whiskey. Ceraso experimented with others: "I have tried it with Jameson's, Bushmills, and Powers. They were too sweet. I chose Redbreast 12 because I needed an Irish whiskey that could stand up to the other ingredients' unique taste profiles. Redbreast fit that bill and added the craft element since it is pot stilled and aged."

The recipe also includes Drambuie to add a honey-based sweetness and Galliano, an Italian liqueur. "I chose Galliano for several reasons. First, the vanilla notes in the elixir blend well with Redbreast and the anise flavor evident in the Westie's finish. Second, Galliano was in its heyday during the reign of Mickey Spillane."

And what better way to top a mob cocktail than with a Bada Bing cherry?

The Westie Cocktail in full splendor, complete with fedora. The drink was developed by author and cocktail expert Fredo Ceraso and includes a brand-specific list of ingredients. Photo credit: Fredo Ceraso.

THE WESTIE

¾ oz. Redbreast 12-year-old Single Pot Still Irish Whiskey
¾ oz. Drambuie
¾ oz. Liquore Galliano L'Autentico
¾ oz. fresh lemon juice
3 drops of Dutch's Colonial Bitters (or Angostura in a pinch)

Combine ingredients in a cocktail shaker, add ice, and shake for 15–20 seconds. Double strain the mixture into a chilled cocktail glass over a Bada Bing Cherry by Tillman Farms.

Patrick Downey

The author of *Legs Diamond: Gangster, Bad Seeds in the Big Apple,* and *Gangster City*, Patrick Downey specializes in stories of wiseguys from the Prohibition era, when drinks were sneaked in speakeasies and many a cocktail recipe was lost to time. Like his subjects, Downey likes the finer things, but also keeps close to his roots.

"'Life is too short to drink cheap wine.' I received that sound piece of advice a few decades ago and have applied that philosophy to both grappa and beer. Therefore it is ironic that my beer of choice is Pabst Blue Ribbon."

While this blue-collar stalwart has in recent years become a hipster favorite, for Downey PBR is anything but trendy.

"Growing up in Detroit, Pabst was the drink of the grandparents and relatives who are now classified as the Greatest Generation. They grew up with nothing so the fact that they had a house, food, and necessities meant life was good. A case of PBR was icing on the cake. They had no car—Detroit buses got them where they needed to go. There were no vacations, no boat, no swimming pool and no complaints.

"I point out what they didn't have, they never mentioned it. What they did have was a good time. There was always laughter. Time spent enjoying

Patrick Downey writes about gangsters. But not just any gangsters. His specialty is the "fedora-wearing, machine-gun-totin', beer-selling kind." Photo credit: Patrick Downey.

each other's company. In the warmer months, hours were spent on a screened-in back porch that was sparsely decorated with a few lawn chairs and tables. There was a radio for any Tiger game that might be on, or, if there were no sports then it was an oldies music station; Glenn Miller, Sinatra, etc. The 'lounge' opened around noon, the beverage of choice—Pabst Blue Ribbon."

Downey's interest in Prohibition-era crime also came from hours spent on that back porch soaking up tales of the 1920s and '30s:

"Over the course of a few PBRs I would hear about my grandma's father, who was a bootlegger. He ran stuff over from Canada, supposedly working with the Purple Gang as well as Capone. I remember one time, after hearing a story about the Purples, asking my grandpa if it was scary living in Detroit at the time. 'Nah,' he said, then, paraphrasing Bugsy Siegel, added, 'they only killed each other.'"

Pabst Blue Ribbon

Downey's favorite beer got its start in Milwaukee in 1843. But it was in 1860, according to the beer's website, that steamship captain Frederick Pabst bought a share in the company. The iconic blue ribbon is said to have been added to the brand after it took top honors in a beer competition in 1882, though the exact details of the event remain murky.

LOS GINTONIC

This recipe, from *Saveur* magazine, adds a bit of dry vermouth to offset the navy gin, which is 57% alcohol (100 proof).

1½ oz. navy-strength gin
½ oz. dry vermouth
3 oz. bitter lemon tonic water
1 strip lemon zest, for garnish

Combine 1½ oz. navy-strength gin and ½ oz. dry vermouth in an ice-filled shaker. Shake vigorously and strain into an old-fashioned glass filled with crushed ice; top with 3 oz. bitter lemon tonic and garnish with lemon zest.

Did you know that during Prohibition Pabst started making cheese to stay in business? In 1930 Pabst sold over 8 million pounds of Pabst-ett cheese.

Gangsters were involved with Pabst breweries as well. In an FBI wiretap from 1962, agents listened in as Chicago gangster Joe Costello told mob boss Sam Giancana that he and another gangster in Chicago Heights "handled all the (Pabst) licenses for the past fifteen or twenty years."

Scott M. Burnstein

Scott M. Burnstein probes the depths of Midwest mob history and the psyche of major mob turncoats. His first book, *Motor City Mafia*, exposed the secrets of the Detroit syndicate. His follow-up, *Family Affair*, focused on another Midwest mob family, the Chicago Outfit, while his *Mafia Prince* tells the story of Phil Leonetti, a Philly Mafia turncoat. Burnstein runs the website Gangster Report and is far ahead of any journalist with the latest developments in the American underworld.

His favorite cocktail is a gin and tonic (Tanqueray, Bombay). "I just think it's cool that it's an old school, no-nonsense kind of drink, much like the people I write about."

Gin and Tonic

So simple, so elegant. A gin and tonic is the ultimate summer cocktail. As straightforward as the cocktail sounds, it can easily be tweaked into a number of satisfying variations. But unlike the joke that novelty vodka martinis have become (appletini?), the unique flavor and complexity of gin keeps these variations well within acceptable limits.

Christian Cipollini tackles well-known gangland subjects (like Lucky Luciano) from a fresh angle. Photo credit: Christian Cipollini.

Christian Cipollini

Another mob expert who prefers traditional cocktails is Christian Cipollini, author of *Diary of a Motor City Hit Man: The Chester Wheeler Campbell Story*, *Lucky Luciano: Mysterious Tales of a Gangland Legend,* and *Murder Inc.: Mysteries of the Mob's Most Deadly Hit Squad.*

"Above all the many cleverly named, and some damn tasty drinks of today, I still find myself drawn to a good dirty martini. When I say 'good'—I mean there are some bad ones, i.e. they serve you a plain martini. Top-shelf gin, Bombay Sapphire is my favorite, at least three or four olives drowning in it, equal parts both dry and sweet vermouth. And don't be conservative on the olive juice!"

Seth Ferranti

Seth Ferranti is a multi-media writer and journalist who pens amazing true crime and prison-related stories for *Vice* and other outlets. He started his career in journalism while incarcerated. In 1993, after spending two years as a top-15 fugitive on the US Marshal's most wanted list, he was captured and sentenced to 304 months under the federal sentencing guidelines for an LSD Kingpin conviction.

A first-time, non-violent offender, Ferranti served twenty-one years of his twenty-five-year mandatory minimum sentence. During his incarceration, Ferranti earned an AA degree from Penn State, a BA degree from the University of Iowa, and an MA from California State University, Dominguez Hills through correspondence courses. He also got an education in behind-bars drinking.

> "They used to make moonshine in prison with potatoes and they had these really elaborate contraptions to make it and they used to trip the breakers all the time when they cooked it up. Also hooch was much more common. It was easier to stash and quicker to make. Mostly homemade alcohol but I was a couple of places where there was real liquor. In FCI Fort Dix you used to see real bottles of Jack Daniel's or Crown Royal or other types of whiskey every now and then. I don't know how it got in but I could imagine someone paid a guard to bring it in. How much? I don't know but probably several hundred for one bottle."

In prison, Ferranti stayed away from alcohol and all the trouble that went with it. ("Too much drama and opportunities to do stupid shit. And one thing about dudes in prison, they don't know where to stop or draw the line.")

Now, he's rediscovering the pleasure, without the drama.

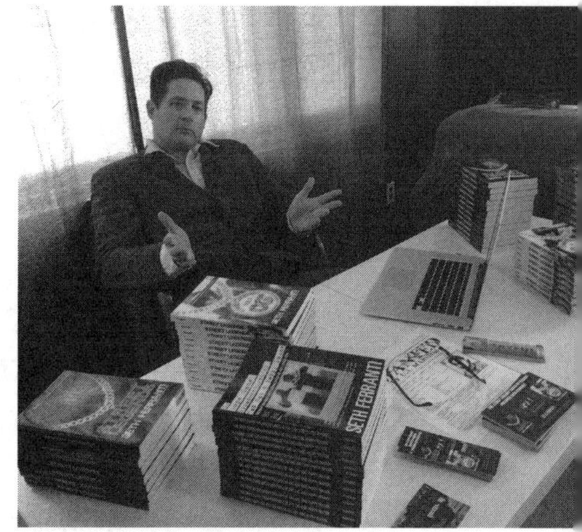

Seth Ferranti began to write in prison and has emerged as one of the leading experts on prison culture and gangs. Photo credit: Seth Ferranti.

> "I like to drink good European beer. I am partial to Samuel Smith's. It is hand brewed in England and can only be found in specialty beer shops. I like the Oatmeal Stout and they got this Chocolate Stout that is awesome. It's the same beer I drank before I went in. I just reconnected with it. I like Stoli's also but haven't had a lot of that since I've been out. Maybe I drank it one time. I don't have a regular bar I go to. Mostly buy the beer and drink at home or I go to Ameristar, the casino here in St. Louis with my wife and we smuggle the beers in to drink while we play the slots. That's about the extent of my illegal activities these days."

Chriss Lyon

Historian and author Chriss Lyon has not only walked the beat, but shot the most famous Thompson submachine guns in the world, all while documenting and researching the Roaring Twenties. Using techniques of forensic genealogy combined with investigative research, she has discovered little-known facts about the people and events surrounding the St. Valentine's Day Massacre, which she details in her book *A Killing in Capone's Playground: The True Story of the Hunt for the Most Dangerous Man Alive*.

"I had the opportunity to uncover some of the actions and dialogue associated with Capone hit man and St. Valentine's Day Massacre suspect, Fred 'Killer' Burke, as reported by witnesses at the time. In 1931, Burke made the comment to a deputy guarding him at the Berrien County, Michigan jail, saying, 'The grape wine here is great.' Of course he was referring to the locally grown fruit crop from Southwestern Michigan's Fruit Belt. His taste for the fermented fruits may also have played a role in his undoing; men accompanying Burke on December 14, 1929 told investigators that he had been consuming wine all day. Later that same evening, Burke shot and killed St. Joseph Patrolman Charles Skelly.

"In the spirit of these long-gone connoisseurs of fermented beverages, I too agree that the 'grape wine here is great.' Two of my favorites are Tabor Hill Winery's Classic Demi-Red and Lake Michigan Shore Riesling."

Gavin Schmitt

Gavin Schmitt is an up-and-coming true crime author. His first book details the rise and fall of one of the more enigmatic Mafia organizations in American history, the Milwaukee Mafia. Schmitt's meticulous research gives the first-ever book on this Wisconsin Mafia organization a heft and depth rarely seen in debut efforts.

Gavin's favorite drinks lean toward the blue collar, fitting for an author who specializes in a Rust Belt city. "Aficionados are going to be disappointed. But I don't drink anything too exotic. My father always enjoyed the bottom-shelf beers, like Boxer and Genesee, and I very much followed in his footsteps. I'd take a PBR or Milwaukee's Best over a craft beer any day. With booze, it's whiskey, preferably scotch. Just last week I enjoyed a bottle of Johnny Walker Black with Bob Murawski, Oscar-winning editor of *The Hurt Locker*. One of the highlights of the year, easily."

CHAPTER 5

Cocktail Noir on Screen

Give me a double bourbon, and leave the bottle.

PI MIKE HAMMER

From the earliest silent films to movies slated for release this year, the crime genre never seems to wane in popularity. As I note throughout this book, mobster stories are a form of noir. But for this chapter, I'll make the distinction between two types of movies: film noir and the gangster movie.

They share some overlapping themes, and indeed many film noirs could also be classified as gangster movies. In film noir, gangsters often appear as the foil to a detective or as the boyfriend of a femme fatale looking to get out of mob life. Both types of movie also prominently feature bars as social gathering spots and drinks as a way to loosen lips or silence them via poison. Liquor often flows freely in both genres, consumed by characters doing everything from celebrating the release of a fellow gangster from prison to entertaining a girlfriend.

Another notable trait these genres share is that they boast movies considered to be among the best ever made. From classic noir's *The Maltese Falcon* to one of the most celebrated films of all time, *The Godfather*, there is something about these stories that attracts the best writers, actors, and directors.

FILM NOIR

The term *film noir* first appeared in 1946 to describe a certain type of dark, shadowy picture filled with characters of questionable morals. There were femme fatales, criminals, and regular guys who got mixed up with them. The movie genre is known for its cinematography: the sharp angles, contrasting light, and use of shadows to create mood.

While the words *film noir* may evoke old black-and-white movies, the genre continues to evolve with modern approaches. Movies from *Red Rock West* and *Fargo* to science fiction flicks like *Dark City* and *Blade Runner* all borrow elements from early film noir and expand the genre past its pulp origins.

Drinking, of course, featured heavily in the film noir golden era. Cocktails were expertly crafted on screen and sipped with an air of sophistication. It was rare to see a binge drinker, though booze was often used for more than taking the edge off or winding down after a hard day chasing criminals or investigating a murder; a cocktail could be the delivery mechanism for poison, or a way to make a wide-eyed innocent more pliable to nefarious influence. The cocktails were strong. Forget sugary pre-made mixes. This was the hard stuff.

SCOTCH MIST

2 oz. scotch

Lemon twist

Fill a glass with crushed ice. Add scotch, twist lemon peel over, and mix in.

The Big Sleep

Bogie and Bacall and Chandler. As cool as it gets.

Here, as in most films of that era, you can tell a lot about a character by what he or she drinks. In one scene, Bacall orders a Scotch Mist. One might think because of its name that the cocktail is light and airy. But it's actually scotch and a twist of lemon on ice. Bacall shows she has the hardboiled edge to basically drink straight scotch, not giving anything up to Bogart.

Bogart, with his swagger, his stare, and the way his hat sits just to the side oozes the confidence a noir hero (or anti-hero) needs. Off screen, Bogart not only enjoyed Scotch, he maintained that booze could end global conflict. In 1950 he opined, "The whole world is three drinks behind. If everyone in the world would take three drinks, we would have no trouble. If Stalin, Truman and everybody else in the world had three drinks right now, we'd all loosen up and we wouldn't need the United Nations."

High Tide

"There's a wonderful B-noir we restored called *High Tide*, a Monogram from 1947," said Eddie Muller, author, and founder of the Film Noir Foundation. "Lee Tracy plays a hard-bitten newspaper editor—what else did he ever play?—and one of the film's subtle pleasures is watching him carefully craft a cocktail. You could tell this guy was a professional drinker. I chose not to believe the legendary story about him getting barred from Mexico in 1933 for pissing off a balcony onto a passing military parade while filming *Viva Villa!* That's an amateur stunt; this guy was clearly a pro."

Wordslinger, impresario, and noirchaelogist Eddie Muller, president of the Film Noir Foundation. Photo credit: Eddie Muller.

While the City Sleeps

This film, directed by Fritz Lang, has an all-star noir cast including Dana Andrews, Ida Lupino, and a pre-horror career Vincent Price. The story centers on the cutthroat world of the newspaper industry. Reporters race to identify a serial murderer known as the Lipstick Killer as part of a competition between three divisions of the paper. The winner gets to run the company.

Drinking sets the ambiance throughout the movie. Reporters gather to gossip in a basement watering hole, where they down whiskey and rum on the rocks. Newspaper magnates savor brandy out of snifters in a posh apartment. Martinis and champagne flow as freely as the dialogue. There seems to be a drink in someone's hand in almost every scene.

CHAMPAGNE BELLINI

2 oz. peach juice
4 oz. champagne (chilled of course)
Add peach juice to a champagne flute, pour champagne on top.

Champagne Bellini
In one memorable scene, Ida Lupino and George Sanders are sitting in a (deliciously kitschy) tiki bar. Sanders is concocting an unusual drink at the table, spinning a huge peach in a flute glass before pouring champagne over the fruit. It looks as if he is making a bellini, though most recipes call for peach juice. Also note that a bellini is more typically made with prosecco (Italian sparkling wine).

DOA
The 1950 version of *DOA* (the film was remade with Dennis Quaid in 1988, but the original is the superior movie) opens with Frank Bigelow, portrayed by Edmond O'Brien, reporting his own murder to police. He was poisoned and the movie unfolds as Bigelow tries to find out who was responsible before he dies.

In one early scene Bigelow is at a business party. He asks, "How about a little bourbon?" and gets a tall glass of the spirit on the rocks.

Soon, his taste for bourbon would prove fatal. The party moves to a hot jazz nightclub, the Fisherman in San Francisco, where Bigelow orders a "bourbon and water, no ice." Unfortunately, he leaves his glass at the other end of the bar and a mysterious man in a checkered topcoat and hat switches it for a drink laced with poison.

1945's *Scarlet Street*, a noir directed by Fritz Lang, starred Edward G. Robinson and Joan Bennett. They previously starred together in the 1944 noir *The Woman in the Window*. Photo credit: author collection.

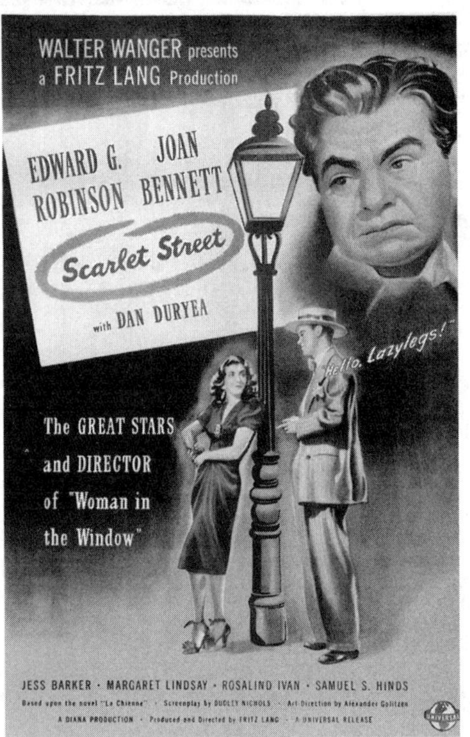

WALTER WANGER presents
a FRITZ LANG Production
EDWARD G. ROBINSON
JOAN BENNETT
Scarlet Street
with DAN DURYEA
"Hello, Lazylegs!"
The GREAT STARS and DIRECTOR of "Woman in the Window"
JESS BARKER · MARGARET LINDSAY · ROSALIND IVAN · SAMUEL S. HINDS
Based upon the novel "La Chienne" · Screenplay by DUDLEY NICHOLS · Art Direction by Alexander Golitzen
A DIANA PRODUCTION · Produced and Directed by FRITZ LANG · A UNIVERSAL RELEASE

Woman in the Window

Edward G. Robinson stars in this 1944 Fritz Lang-directed noir about a college professor, Richard Wanley, who finds himself involved with a devious femme fatale named Alice, portrayed by Joan Bennett. Cocktails play a part in some of the movie's pivotal scenes. When Richard first meets Alice outside a bar, she gives him the line that sinks him. "I'm not married, I have no designs on you, and one drink is all I care for." The next scene is set in a swank 1940s nightclub, complete with white-tux waiters. Drinks flow as Richard finds himself becoming more intoxicated with liquor and Alice's charms. From there the camera moves to Alice's apartment, where, as she and the professor share a bottle of champagne, her husband comes home, and Richard stabs him.

In one scene, Alice faces a blackmailer who threatens to expose her involvement in the murder. While he's confronting her, she casually mixes up a couple of scotch and sodas. She knows she's in deep, but she won't be easily intimidated.

WOMAN IN THE WINDOW SCOTCH AND SODA

2½ oz. scotch

Seltzer

Pour 2½ oz. of scotch in a highball glass. Fill glass halfway with seltzer. Add one ice cube. Don't mix. Give to blackmailer.

Scarlet Street

With the same main cast as *Woman in the Window*, this 1945 film noir also features some cocktail scenes that add essential plot points to the movie. Edward G. Robinson plays a mild-mannered painter who gets caught up in a deception orchestrated by Joan Bennett's character. In one of the early scenes, they walk into a basement bar and Robinson orders a Rum Collins, hoping to impress Bennett with his sophisticated tastes.

RUM COLLINS

2 oz. rum

2 oz. club soda

¾ oz. lemon juice

¾ oz. simple syrup

Lemon slice

Add first four ingredients to a shaker filled with ice. Shake vigorously. Pour into ice-filled glass and garnish with lemon slice.

The Breaking Point

This 1950 noir is an adaptation of Hemingway's *To Have and Have Not.* Not as well-known as the 1944 version featuring Bogart, this one has a pivotal bar scene with rich dialogue. John Garfield plays Harry Morgan, a fishing boat captain down on his luck. He reluctantly gets involved in shady dealings to keep his business going and to provide for his family. He also starts to fall under the spell of a femme fatale, Leona Charles, played by Patricia Neal.

When Morgan first meets Charles at a bar she requests a daiquiri while he orders a curt, "Two beers." They drink over some classic noir banter.

CHARLES: Don't you want to be friendly?

MORGAN: Sure I want to be friendly. My wife wouldn't like it.

CHARLES: You're kidding.

MORGAN: No.

CHARLES: Oh so you're one of those. I don't meet many. Is she pretty?

MORGAN: She's got something for me.

Kiss Me Deadly

Based on Mickey Spillane's book of the same name, 1955's *Kiss Me Deadly* came at the end of the golden age of noir, but it ranks as one of the absolute best films in the genre. From its inventive opening sequence (a car racing down the road with the backward title sequence rolling by to not only music, but a woman sobbing) to the memorable finale (not going to spoil it), *Deadly* is a mix of classic noir tropes and the mid-1950s obsession with all things atomic. From bourbon to beer, drinks flow throughout the movie. While the drink scenes are not key plot points, they do much to flesh out the characters, especially PI Mike Hammer. In one scene, Hammer walks into a bar and says, "Give me a double bourbon, and leave the bottle." That one line says a lot.

My Gun Is Quick

Two years after *Kiss Me Deadly*, Hammer returned to the screen in *My Gun Is Quick*. As in the earlier movie, there are lots of scenes in nightclubs, with walls of bottles serving as the backdrop for conversations. When offered a drink at one club, Hammer replies, "Double bourbon. Straight." A club patron orders a double bourbon for himself and Hammer, while two female companions order "vodka Smirnoff's," which come to them as vodka straight, no ice.

Dial 1119

In this lesser-known noir, a killer takes hostages in a bar. In one scene, Chuckles the bartender (yes, Chuckles the bartender) says he's going to the back for "some more vermouth." Instead he heads straight to the phone to call the police. He is promptly shot in the back while dialing the phone. He should have stuck to the vermouth.

RAMOS GIN FIZZ

This classic New Orleans cocktail dates back to the 1880s. Mixing the drink is time-consuming but worth it. This version from *Food Republic* is similar to the recipe used at the Roosevelt Hotel in New York City.

2 oz. gin (London Dry or Old Tom)
1 oz. heavy cream
1 oz. simple syrup
½ oz. fresh squeezed lemon juice
½ oz. fresh squeezed lime juice
1 egg white
3 dashes orange blossom water
1 drop vanilla extract (optional)

Combine ingredients and dry shake for 10 seconds without ice. Add several small to medium-sized ice cubes and shake hard for several minutes. Continue shaking as long as you are able and until you can no longer hear the ice inside. Pour foamy contents into a chilled Collins glass and slowly top with soda to raise the head.

The Blue Dahlia

Written for the screen by Raymond Chandler, this 1946 film follows a WWII veteran (played by Alan Ladd) as he and the police search for the killer of his wife, who was busy partying and seeing other men while he was off at war. As she tells him when he surprises her after coming home, "I take all the drinks I want. Any time. Any place."

The opening scene sets the importance of spirits to the plot of the movie. Coming off a bus, a WWII veteran, played by William Bendix, spies a cocktail lounge. He asks his friend Johnny (Alan Ladd) to stop for a goodbye drink. Ladd responds, "Why not? One bar is just like another." Bendix exclaims, "as long as they have bourbon," to which a third friend (Hugh Beaumont) opines, "or a reasonable facsimile." Walking into the bar, the men order "a bourbon with a bourbon chaser." It's in this opening scene where you see the deep camaraderie between the men, as well as William Bendix's PTSD. Both come into play as the movie goes on, as Bendix becomes one of the murder suspects.

Other scenes revolve around booze-soaked house parties, broken bottles at a murder scene, and The Blue Dahlia, a nightclub.

Dead Reckoning

Humphrey Bogart and Lizabeth Scott star in this 1947 film noir. Bogart plays a war hero who investigates the death of a fellow paratrooper. When he digs into his friend's past he comes up against murder, blackmail, and (you guessed it) a femme fatale. The plot is complex and a challenge to follow, just like the recipe for the Ramos Gin Fizz that Scott's character imbibes.

RYE AND WATER

It's difficult to picture a tough guy like Bogart waiting around for a gin fizz. So, appropriately, he orders a simple rye and water in the movie.

2 oz. rye
2 oz. water

Add to glass with ice. Stir and garnish with lemon peel.

ROBERT MITCHUM'S EGGNOG

From Frank DeCaro's *Christmas in Tinseltown*. Mitchum's off-screen drinking was notorious, as were his fights and brushes with the law. This recipe for eggnog is, no surprise, stronger than a standard eggnog.

12 egg yolks
1 pound confectioners' sugar
1 quart rum, brandy, or whiskey
2 quarts cream
1 quart milk
12 egg whites
½ teaspoon salt

Beat egg yolks and confectioners' sugar together in a large bowl. Beat in the rum, brandy, or whiskey. Add cream and milk. In a separate bowl, beat egg whites with salt until stiff but not dry. Fold this mixture into the liquid. Chill. Serves 20.

Robert Mitchum

One of Hollywood's leading tough guys, Mitchum starred in a number of film noir and gangster movies during his long career. His sleepy-eyed, steely persona fit perfectly with many of his memorable characters. In the noir classic *Out of the Past* Mitchum's private investigator, Jeff, wanders through the labyrinth plot, cigarette dangling out of his mouth. Mitchum's narration of the movie just bleeds classic noir:

> "I knew I'd go every night until she showed up. I knew she knew it. I sat there and drank bourbon and I shut my eyes, but I didn't think of a joint on 56th Street. I knew where I was and what I was doing . . . what a sucker I was. I even knew she wouldn't come the first night. But I sat there, grinding it out."

One of Mitchum's greatest roles (in my opinion) is in one of the most underrated crime/gangster/modern noir movies ever (not my opinion, scientific fact), *The Friends of Eddie Coyle*. Doused in 1970s grittiness, Mitchum plays Eddie Fingers, a weary, low- level Boston hood who becomes an informant for the cops after he's busted transporting hijacked liquor. His target is Dillon, a bar owner and mob hood. Grimy, dingy bars serving cheap beer in crappy glasses are essential to the style and feel of the movie. After getting drunk at a Bruins game with Dillon, Eddie passes out in a car. Dillon's already planning to kill Eddie for snitching. A lot of beer just makes the job easier.

Boris Karloff

There are few images more recognizable than a picture of Boris Karloff in full Frankenstein monster makeup. The actor's name might not be as familiar to younger moviegoers, but everyone knows the square-headed, bolt-necked monster (often erroneously referred to simply as "Frankenstein"). Karloff is best known as a horror movie actor, from his roles in *The Black Cat*, *The Mummy*, and dozens of other high- (and low-) budget scare-fests from the 1930s through the 1960s.

But Karloff also appeared in crime dramas, from the early pulp flick *The Public Defender* to the 1947 film noir *Lured* (which also starred a young Lucille Ball). He even had a small role in the seminal gangster film, 1932's *Scarface*.

BORIS KARLOFF COCKTAIL

¾ ounce gin
¾ oz. St-Germain (or other elderflower liqueur)
1 ounce fresh lime juice
1 tablespoon confectioners' sugar
1 large egg white
Ice
1 ounce chilled club soda
Pinch each of finely grated lime zest and freshly ground pepper, for garnish.

In a cocktail shaker, combine the gin, elderflower liqueur, lime juice, sugar, and egg white. Shake well. Add ice and shake again. Strain into an ice-filled Collins glass, stir in the club soda, and garnish with the lime zest and pepper.

Boris Karloff Cocktail

Chef Todd Thrasher created this supremely tasty cocktail. First looking at the recipe, you might be turned off by the raw egg white. But the shaking action with the alcohol takes care of any salmonella worries and results in a full and frothy cocktail. The name comes from one of the ingredients, elderberry liqueur. Boris Karloff starred in the original stage version of *Arsenic and Old Lace.* In the play, two elderly sisters poison lonely old men with elderberry wine.

GANGSTER MOVIES

Gangster movies have been around since the invention of moving pictures. Silent films that touched on gangland themes emerged in the early 1900s, though they often had a Wild West plot. The public was not yet quite aware of the real underworld and how it was growing and changing. Only a few years later, Prohibition brought tales of gangsters to newspapers and magazines across the country. Hollywood soon followed.

It was James Cagney and Edward G. Robinson who took the gangster movie to the next level. Their 1930s works from *Little Caesar* to *White Heat* set the standard for underworld films. Over the next couple of decades, gangster movies usually followed the title character's rise and inevitable fall, rarely offering a chance at redemption. By the 1960s, the gangster genre was getting a little stale. That would change in the early 1970s with the release of *The Godfather I* and *II*, followed by Martin Scorsese's *Mean Streets*. The gangster film would never be the same. The violence was more realistic, the dialogue richer, and the blood, well, redder.

Gangster films and TV shows didn't just reflect what was going on in society. They actually influenced real-life gangsters. Starting with Cagney's early movies, hoods would imitate the swagger, clothing, and accents of their on-screen counterparts. As the films inspired the mobsters to act a certain way, that reinforced the movie-going public's image of gangsters. But it was *The Godfather* that cemented the relationship between pop culture and the underworld. Mario Puzo's novel and Marlon Brando's on-screen depiction of Vito Corleone were based on real-life godfathers, bosses from Carlo Gambino to Sam DeCavalcante.

Perhaps the ultimate marriage of pop culture and organized crime came in Scorsese's 1995 classic, *Casino*. In one scene, a hit man has to chase and gun down a target of mob justice. The technical advisor on the movie was Frank Culotta, a real-life Vegas gangster who was part of the Hole-in-the-Wall Gang (led by Tony Spilotro) played in the movie by Joe Pesci. Frank told Scorsese that the murder did not happen the way it was being filmed. And he knew. He committed the murder in real life. So instead of an actor, Frank stepped in and was filmed reenacting the hit as he'd done it in real life.

It wasn't just big-screen mob portrayals that got the attention of the underworld. In the early 2000s, when the FBI was reinvestigating the New Jersey–based Decavalcante family, agents listened on wiretaps as members of the crime family discussed, at length, the similarities between themselves and characters on the HBO show *The Sopranos*. The line between fact and fiction blurred as aging wiseguys wondered aloud about the inspiration behind some of the main characters and debated who should play who.

The *Godfather* Trilogy

The Godfather is not only one of the most celebrated gangster movies ever, but one of the true classics in all of cinema. Along with *The Godfather Part II,* the saga of the Corleone family gave pop culture characters and quotes that still resonate. While *Part III* failed to live up to the first two films, when viewed in tandem, it holds up fairly well.

The *Godfather* movies paint the Mafia in a glamorous haze. Even the killings, from the subtle (Tessio's fate) to the over-the-top (Sonny's final ride at the toll booth), are presented as poetic pieces of a Greek tragedy. The gritty, street-level view is far from the inner circle of the Corleone family, even during flashbacks to their early years in the immigrant slums of New York City. *The Godfather* created its own mythos, which still permeates pop culture.

Wine is integral to all the *Godfather* movies. It's the obvious beverage of choice. While *The Godfather* is about a crime organization, it's also about family, specifically a first- and second-generation Italian-American family. Wine is an essential part of dinners, parties, and conversations. Growing up in a Portuguese family (maternal side), I was surrounded by relatives and family friends who were first-generation Americans. I can tell you from personal experience that gallons of red wine (generally homemade) would be consumed over meals. It was part of the culture. Fittingly, *Godfather* director Francis Ford Coppola owns a large winery in California.

Wine flows throughout the opening wedding scene of *The Godfather*. One of the Corleone family's top lieutenants, Clemenza, breathing heavily from dancing, calls out, "Bring me some wine." In another scene, when the Corleone family is in hiding due to a mob war (i.e. hitting the mattresses), Michael is shown how to make proper Italian sauce, adding the red wine.

CLASSIC CHAMPAGNE COCKTAIL

The champagne cocktail is also featured in the *Thin Man* movies and in the novel *The Big Sleep*, where General Sternwood describes his ideal champagne cocktail as having "a third of a glass of brandy under the Champagne and the Champagne cold as Valley Forge. Colder if you can get it colder."

2–3 dashes Angostura bitters
1 sugar cube
Champagne
Lemon twist

Add bitters to sugar cube. Top with champagne and add lemon twist.

In one of the key scenes between an aging Vito Corleone and his son Michael, the elder don makes way for the younger man to ascend to the family throne. He gives his son business advice, telling him who to look out for. The conversation veers into a brief personal exchange, a moment that hints at the deeper father-son relationship.

VITO: I like to drink wine more than I used to.
MICHAEL: It's good for you, Pop.
VITO: Anyway I'm drinking more.

Choice of drink also underscores a pivotal plot line from *The Godfather Part II.* Michael Corleone's empire is threatened by a high-ranking capo, Frank Patangali, who defects and turns government informant. In this exchange, the disgruntled capo attempts to show how the godfather has lost touch with the common mobsters in his syndicate:

FRANK: Michael, you're sitting high up in the Sierra Mountains and you're drinking . . . . What's he drinking?
CHI-CHI: Champagne.
FRANKIE: Champagne. Champagne cocktails! And you're passing judgment on how I run my family.

Get Carter

British gangster films have their own style and feel, different from those of US mob movies. But in these, too, booze plays a part. One of the greats, 1971's *Get Carter*, features Michael Caine as a mobster who travels from London back to his hometown to find out more about the death of his brother. The film's bleak setting, a gritty Newcastle, adds to the noir feel of the movie. Jack Carter's brother apparently died in a drunk driving accident. But Jack finds out that his brother was murdered by being forced to drink a bottle of whiskey. Jack gets his revenge by, in turn, pouring a bottle of whiskey down the killer's mouth. Jack then beats him to death.

Goodfellas

The day-to-day life of a mobster is hardly as glamorous as portrayed on screen. There is a lot of scraping by, of small-time scores and bookmaking at the neighborhood bar. That day-to-day struggle is reflected in the mob masterpiece *Goodfellas,* based on the true life story of mobster Henry Hill. The movie features a number of key scenes at bars and nightclubs.

MILK PUNCH

There are a variety of milk punch recipes, from those using bourbon to others using rum, brandy, or cognac. The basic ingredients are spirits, milk, sugar, vanilla, and a variety of spices. This is a New Orleans brandy milk punch recipe.

2 oz. brandy (bourbon is also commonly used.)
1 cup whole milk
1 teaspoon powdered sugar
3 ice cubes
Cracked ice
Freshly grated nutmeg

In a cocktail shaker, combine the brandy, milk, and sugar with 3 ice cubes and shake until frothy, about 1 minute. Strain into a double old-fashioned glass with cracked ice. Sprinkle with nutmeg and serve.

STARDUST COCKTAIL

One of the many casinos that the mob had control over was the Stardust. This cocktail is light and purple hued, probably not what a bruiser like Tony Spilotro or Fat Herbie Blitzstein would order.

½ oz. Absolut Citron vodka
½ oz. peach schnapps
½ oz. Blue Curaçao liqueur
1 oz. sweet and sour mix
1 oz. pineapple juice
1 splash grenadine syrup

Fill shaker cup with ice. Pour in all ingredients. Shake and strain into glass.

Whether they are partying, scheming, or killing, the mobsters in the movie always have a drink in hand. They meet at the local neighborhood watering hole to plot their crimes, including one based on the real-life 1978 Lufthansa heist that netted the mob millions of dollars and was for a long time the largest robbery in New York City history.

There is, of course, the famous Steadicam shot of Henry and Karen Hill (Ray Liotta and Lorraine Bracco) entering the Copacabana. But there are also scenes in underground gambling dens and the tropical-themed Bamboo Lounge bar where Tommy DeVito (Joe Pesci) has his famous "What am I, a clown?" scene.

But one of the most intense bar scenes takes place in the fictional Suite Lounge, where Billy Batts is celebrating his return from prison. Tommy walks in to meet up with Henry and Jimmy (Robert DeNiro). He sees Billy and they get into a tense verbal spat, ending with Billy Batts's taunting line, "Now go home and get your fucking shine box." The next scene has Tommy returning to the bar after storming out, and with help from Henry and Jimmy, stomping and beating Billy to death on the barroom floor.

Guys and Dolls

This Tony award-winning play was made into a movie in 1955. While it's not a true gangster movie, it features mobsters, played by Frank Sinatra and Marlon Brando. One scene has Brando ordering a milk punch. He mentions to Jean Simmons that they sometime add Bacardi to the milk. When she asks if Bacardi has alcohol in it, Brando replies, "Just enough to stop the milk from turning sour."

Casino

Robert DeNiro teamed up again with Martin Scorsese and Joe Pesci for this 1995 film about the rise and fall of Lefty Rosenthal and the Chicago Outfit's hold on Las Vegas. It concentrates on the "skim," the long-running mob operation that siphoned millions of dollars from Las Vegas casinos in the '70s and early '80s. The movie was a snapshot of Old Vegas as much as of the final stand of traditional organized crime in Sin City. While the mob may have helped build the city, they also stole from it.

DONNIE BRASCO COCKTAIL

This cocktail, from Drinks Mixer website, is rich and flavorful, perfect for a cold dark night at a mob bar.

1 oz. Bailey's Irish Cream
1 oz. coffee liqueur
1 oz. dark rum
1 oz. Irish whiskey

Mix all ingredients in a glass over ice.

THE LEFT HAND

This cocktail, created in 2007 by New York bartender Sam Ross, is named after Benjamin "Lefty" Ruggerio, Pacino's character in the movie. The drink is similar in construction to a Boulevardier, with the addition of mole bitters.

2 oz. bourbon
¾ oz. sweet vermouth
¾ oz. Campari
2 dashes Xocolatl Mole bitters

Mix all ingredients with ice in a shaker. Stir for 30 seconds and drain into a glass.

7 AND 7

2 oz. Seagram's 7
7-Up
Lemon or lime wedge
Pour the Seagram's 7 into a highball glass filled with ice. Add 7-Up. Garnish with wedge.

MEAN STREETS

From the Laszlo Bar in San Francisco, this drink is an homage to the film.
Half a lemon, cut into quarters
1½ oz. Sambuca
½ oz. rye whiskey
Muddle the lemon quarters in a cocktail shaker. Add the Sambuca and ice and shake. Strain into a rocks glass filled with crushed ice and float rye whiskey over the top. Garnish with a lemon twist and fresh mint.

Donnie Brasco

One of the great mob movie classics is 1997's *Donnie Brasco*, based on the true story of undercover FBI agent Joe Pistone (played by Johnny Depp), who infiltrates the Bonnano crime family in the late 1970s. The action moves from New York City to Florida (Tampa in real life, Miami in the movie). Director Mike Newell shoots many scenes in bars and social clubs. One of the first scenes, in which Johnny Depp meets Al Pacino, takes place at the Mulberry Street Bar in Little Italy.

For Newell, it seems to be a case of directing what you know. One night he sat down for dinner with Pacino, actor Bruno Kirby, and a group of real-life New York gangsters (including the onetime underboss of the Genovese crime family, Jimmy Ida). According to accounts, Newell got into a drinking contest with one of the wiseguys and managed to drink him under the table.

Mean Streets

Martin Scorsese's first cinematic foray into mob life was 1973's *Mean Streets,* a portrait of low-level mobsters and neighborhood guys in New York City's Little Italy. Starring Robert DeNiro and Harvey Keitel, *Streets* is one of the archetypical modern mob movies. As in other Scorsese films, food and drink play an important role in the lives of the characters. Much of the action takes place in underground nightclubs and the dark, dive bars of Mulberry Street, the heart of the neighborhood.

One of the most famous scenes shows a visibly drunk Harvey Keitel staggering through his party, stopping to take a shot, and then finally passing out on the floor. The camera view, focused tightly on Keitel's face and stumbling with his every move, is often imitated.

Drinks abound, from shots of Southern Comfort to the 7 and 7 DeNiro's character drinks. (The actor ordered the same cocktail in *Goodfellas*. Typecasting?)

Banshee

The *Banshee* Cinemax series follows a thief, recently out of jail, who tracks down his old partners in crime, including his girlfriend (daughter of a Russian mob boss), to a small town in Pennsylvania.

BANSHEE

Okay, so this is not actually a drink named after the show. In fact, it's hard to imagine any of the characters ordering a poolside cocktail like a Banshee. But in the spirit of inclusion . . .

1 oz. banana liqueur
½ oz. crème de cacao liqueur
Cream or milk

Add the liqueurs to a shaker filled with crushed ice. Shake vigorously for 30 seconds. Add to glass with ice. Top with cream.

FILM NOIR COCKTAIL

1½ oz. Grey Goose vodka
¼ oz. cinnamon syrup
¼ oz. berry syrup
3 oz. pineapple juice

Mix all ingredients in shaker with ice. Strain into martini glass.

Through a series of intersecting events, he takes on the identity of the new sheriff in town and integrates himself into the community and his old flame's life. He also comes into conflict with a renegade Native American gang and a local Amish crime boss. There are also Salvadoran drug gangs, a blind Philly gangster, lots of nudity (it's on "Skinemax" after all), and copious amounts of blood.

Many scenes take place at Sugar's bar, owned by an ex-fighter. And though plenty of drinks of indeterminate ingredients are downed, a favorite of almost everyone in the show is Blanton's Single-Barrel bourbon. Blanton's has a signature round bottle with a horse and rider on the stopper.

Film Noir Cocktail

This cocktail, featuring Grey Goose vodka, was created by bartender Nitin Terawi, an "ambassador" for Grey Goose, for the company's 2013 Style Du Jour fashion event. Like the Banshee, it might be a little sweet for Bogie or Bacall. But you have to love the name.

CHAPTER 6

Real-Life Gangsters

Mobsters would always get free drinks, but loved to tip extravagantly so the drinks would end up costing more just because of their big tips, which fed more free drinks, which fed more big tips and so on.

UNDERCOVER FBI MOB INFILTRATOR JACK GARCIA

Christmastime in The Big Apple is a sprawling, dizzying sensory overload for even the most battle-hardened New Yorker. Office parties are in high gear, and that means a lot of liquor. The week before Christmas 1958 was especially good to the employees and customers of the Seambinding Company. Located in the heart of the Garment Center, Seambinding was owned by James "Jimmy Doyle" Plumeri, a capo in the Lucchese crime family, one of New York City's venerable Five Families. Plumeri was one of the main forces in the mob's control of the garment industry in New York City, a hold it maintained for the better part of the twentieth century.

But while Jimmy Doyle used his tough personality and iron-fisted image to grow his business on the street, he knew the value of

THE GANGSTER MARTINI

This recipe, from *The Cooking Bride* website, is a variation on one of the many *Sopranos*-themed martinis.

1 oz. Tuaca
1 oz. amaretto
1 oz. vodka
1½ oz. pineapple juice
Maraschino cherries for garnish

Fill a shaker with ice cubes. Pour in liqueurs, vodka, and pineapple juice. Cover with a tight-fitting lid and shake until combined. Pour into a chilled glass. Garnish with cherries if desired.

CORPSE REVIVER 1

2 oz. cognac
1 oz. apple brandy
1 oz. sweet vermouth

Add ingredients to mixing glass with ice. Stir. Strain into chilled cocktail glass.

treating his employees and customers right. What better way to show gratitude than booze, and lots of it? In the days before Christmas, Plumeri sent one of his employees to start stockpiling supplies for a holiday party. Over the course of seven days, the mobster purchased eight cases of Seagram's VO, two cases of Harvey's Scotch, and one case of Canadian Club. There was little doubt it would all be consumed.

From the early days of organized criminals in America through the various modern crime syndicates, gangsters have thrived in the vice business. Vice—whether liquor, drugs, or gambling—fuels their enterprise. And more often than not, gangsters indulge in as much vice as they sell. In Japan, the feared Yakuza (the largest organized crime group in the world) actually has an ailment named for them. The Yakuza Disease results from years of hard drinking and eating rich foods. For American mobsters, booze isn't associated with illness, but with socializing, celebrating, scheming—and showing off.

The Corpse Reviver Cocktails

The last thing a gangster wants is one of his hits to come back from a near miss. It's happened more often than you think. Mobsters like Fat Pete Chiodo, Ken Eto, and John Veasey became government informants after unsuccessful attempts on their lives. These concoctions are supposed to revive gangsters after another kind of "hit," the one that comes from spending too much time at the bar the night before. The Reviver 1 still shows up on cocktail menus, though the Reviver 2 is more common.

Jay Deitche with his favorite cocktail, Canadian Club on the rocks. Photo credit: author collection.

John L. Deitche

John Deitche, known as Jay, was my paternal grandfather. He was born and lived in Perth Amboy, a city on Raritan Bay in Central New Jersey, just a short bridge ride away from Staten Island. Jay was an ironworker in Local 373 by day and a semi-successful bookie by night. From post-WWII through the mid-1970s, Jay ran a small bookmaking operation with a couple of friends, one of which had ties to organized crime figures. Jay's downfall came in 1972 at the Gay Nineties, a popular bar and bookie hangout in nearby South Amboy. He asked a pretty woman at the bar if she was interested in betting with him. Little did he know she was an undercover

CORPSE REVIVER 2

1 oz. gin
1 oz. Lillet Blanc
1 oz. Cointreau
1 oz. fresh lemon juice
1 dash absinthe
Orange peel for garnish

Add ingredients to shaker with ice. Shake vigorously. Strain into chilled cocktail glass. Garnish with orange peel.

NJ State Trooper. He walked outside the bar and into the waiting arms of the cops.

My grandfather did not want his neighbors to think he was a criminal, so he hired a real estate lawyer to represent him in court. As you can imagine, it did not go well. He was quickly declared guilty. Though Jay made a play for leniency by mentioning that he served in WWII, the judge, unmoved, sentenced him to a year and a day in Trenton State Prison. He served less than a year and gave up his bookmaking operation for good.

So maybe it's in my blood, this fascination with crime. Though, unlike my grandfather, I'd rather write about it than participate. As for his other trait, a fondness for hanging out in bars, I definitely inherited that.

Canadian Club on the Rocks

Jay's favorite drink was a Canadian Club on the rocks, a popular choice in the 1950s and '60s (as evidenced by its frequent appearances on *Mad Men*). Canadian blended whiskeys were first widely consumed in the US during Prohibition. Though whiskey aficionados tend to sneer at Canadian Club (along with many Canadian whiskeys), Jim Beam acquired the spirit a few years ago, banking on a retro comeback.

Jack Garcia

Few undercover FBI agents have penetrated the Mafia as deeply as Jack Garcia. Using the alias Jack Falcone, this Cuban agent passed himself off as an Italian mob associate, cultivating an image and persona so believable mobster Gregory DePalma planned to propose inducting him into the Gambino crime family.

While undercover, Garcia witnessed how mobsters love to mix business with socializing. "We went out to eat a lot. We would all get together at Ruth's Chris in White Plains, Angelo's in Pelham and City Island. Greg DePalma loved good wine and he loved to brag about his wine expertise. The one wine I remember him drinking was Brunello di Montalcino. In fact, he enjoyed any of the Banfi wines. Some of the other mobsters like scotch and water. I know Robert Vaccaro liked to drink scotch," Garcia said.

Garcia also got a course in gangster etiquette. "Mobsters always order drinks by a brand—never just a scotch and water. It would be a Cutty and water or Johnny Walker and water. And no one ever drank out of a straw. That was a big no-no. Mobsters would always get free drinks, but loved to tip extravagantly so the drinks would end up costing more just because of their big tips, which fed more free drinks, which fed more big tips and so on. But for a wiseguy it didn't matter. To them the best drink is the one you get for free. One other thing is that mob guys never got too drunk. They would drink just enough, but you never saw them acting out of control."

Moderate drinking didn't necessarily mean moderate spending. When Garcia was working his operation, infamous Gambino crime family boss John Gotti had long since been sentenced to prison. But the guys around DePalma talked about how Gotti liked to give the capos bottles of Rémy Martin Louis XIII Cognac. With bottles starting around a couple thousand and rising in price to over $10,000, the cognac was a nice gesture of respect from Gotti to his underlings.

Gotti's love for the finer things was confirmed by James Fox, the onetime head of the FBI's New York field office. After Gotti was sentenced to life in prison in 1992, the FBI went to work, trying to trace all the money funneled through the Gambino crime family. There was far less than they thought. As Fox put it, "Gotti and the others also spent a lot on drinking, gambling, and girlfriends." Much of that, no doubt, went to glasses and bottles of Louis XIII.

Garcia has somewhat less extravagant tastes. He enjoys a Ketel One martini with three olives or a Bacardi and Coke (known in the Cuban community as a *Cuba libre*). When it comes to beer, he prefers Beck's.

Mark Silverman

Mark Silverman, former Boston underworld figure who recounts his involvement with the Mafia and the Winter Hill Gang during the

New England mob wars of the 1990s in his book, *Rogue Mobster*, has a preferred drink suited to his former profession: "My favorite cocktail is served after the meal and it's called a Sicilian Kiss. You can order it hot or cold, but a real Sicilian wiseguy always like it hot. I always enjoyed dinner at (imprisoned Boston mobster) Paul DeCologero's favorite restaurant, Lucia's in Winchester. Although Paul could dine wherever he wanted in the North End, he enjoyed Lucia's. I never knew if it was a good or bad whenever we dined together. But I do know he never raised a cold Sicilian kiss to me."

SICILIAN KISS

A popular gangland cocktail, the Sicilian Kiss is easy to mix.

½ oz. Southern Comfort
½ oz. amaretto.

Mix the Southern Comfort and amaretto and pour into a shot glass. Some recipes have the Kiss with a beer chaser, but most let it be on its own.

Sonny Girard

Former New York gangster Sonny Girard turned to writing mob-focused fiction after a RICO conviction sent him to prison for seven years. His books include *Snake Eyes, Sins of Our Sons,* and *Sonny Girard's Mob Reader,* a collection of true and fictional stories. His drinking habits have evolved along with his career.

"I used to drink Rémy Martin in the old days when I was hanging out at bars," he said. "Today I generally only have wine with dinner. I like dry reds like Nero D'Avila, Chianti, or Amarone; with fish, Lacryma Christi."

Chianti is a favorite mobster wine. As sommelier Erin Kane observed, "It's really no wonder. Chianti is the most iconic wine of Italy. It is easy to drink, and meant to be enjoyed with great Italian food like pastas and robust red sauces. Like their neighbors in France and Spain, Italians craft their wine to express the unique terroir of the place the grapes are grown and harvested. Italians love Chianti because when they drink it, it takes them home."

Before Girard went straight, his nighttime activities, like those of most wiseguys, revolved around bars.

"There was a time when we would get arrested at the Cocoa Poodle and it would make headlines," Girard said. "The following weekend, the bar would be packed with females looking to meet mob guys. Some even came with guys who they'd dump if a guy from the bar gave them a turn. One girl came from Jersey on a bicycle. As a young man brought up to believe in 'good girls,' I got a sometimes shocking awakening to the nature of many females."

Steve Lenehan

Steve Lenehan was an associate in the New Jersey underworld for twenty years before wearing a wire on fellow mobsters in the early 1990s. Lenehan socialized and did business with wiseguys from all five New York mob families and members of the Newark faction of the Philly-based Bruno-Scarfo family.

Lenehan's go-to drink was Stoli with a dash of Diet Coke. "I used to say that it was the fruit of the gods—every essential vitamin including zinc."

Sometimes, he overdid it on the zinc. "I used to call it a Riggio morning. My buddy Ray and I had a code after drinking too much the day before and needing a wake up drink at 5 a.m. An old friend, Frank Riggio, owned a sawdust joint on Garden Ave in Belleville. He got there at 4:30 a.m. We'd walk in and Frank would just put a bottle of blackberry brandy on the bar. Ray and I would polish it off, ready for another day of scuffling."

Gerry Chili

One of Lenehan's underworld associates was Bonnano mobster Gerry Chili. "Chili used to say, whenever we went out on the town, 'Let's bust open the liver a bit,'" Lenahan recalled.

"One time in the late eighties we were coming back from the Bronx. It was a hot summer night so we cross over the bridge and are driving through Harlem. Gerry has to take a leak so he says, 'I know this place.' He didn't. So we stop at this bar and we walk in. Gerry has on a seersucker short set, white Bally shoes with no socks, 10-pound gold chain hanging from his neck, and Oleg Cassini shades. We walk in this bar and it was like that scene in *Animal House* when the kids walk into that black bar to see Otis Day. Every-

Sam "Momo" Giancana, boss of the Chicago Outfit and fan of dark shades. Giancana was shot and killed in his basement cooking sausages in 1975. Photo credit: author collection.

one stopped what they were doing and just looked at us. Gerry goes to the bartender, 'Give me a Smirnoff with tonic and give all these brothers a drink with me.' Gerry throws a hundred on the bar. Fifteen minutes later we knew everyone in there. He was the best wiseguy I ever knew."

Sam Giancana

Sam "Momo" Giancana was one of the most powerful and feared mobsters the Windy City had seen since Capone. As the head of the Chicago Outfit, Giancana oversaw a long list of rackets and street crimes. He was linked to a string of paramours from Judith Campbell Exner (who was also having an affair with John F. Kennedy) to Marilyn Monroe (who *also* was having an affair with Kennedy). He became involved in the CIA-backed assassination plots against Fidel Castro, was exiled to Mexico, and was murdered right before he was due to testify to the House Select Committee on Assassinations, which was investigating possible mob involvement in the shooting of President Kennedy.

Law enforcement's constant surveillance of Giancana turned up some nuggets about what cocktails powerful gangsters enjoyed. In one recording, the FBI listened in as Giancana, mobsters Chuckie English and Keely Smith, and another (unidentified) person were hanging out in a Chicago bar. English ordered drinks for the group. He requested four martinis, specifying that they be prepared with Tanqueray "or if not that, then Beefeaters."

John Alite

For over twenty years, John Alite was a close friend and associate of John Gotti Jr. Growing up in Queens, in the shadow of the Gambino crime family, Alite became enamored of the wiseguy life. By the early 1990s he was part of a crew of Gambino mobsters operating in New York and Tampa, Florida. When he was indicted and learned the Gambinos were cutting ties with him, Alite decided to flip and become a government witness. Now he does speaking engagements, warning kids about the perils of a life in crime. He's given up his wiseguy ways, though he admits to keeping one habit from the old days—"I drink martinis with Bombay Sapphire Gin."

Steven Maggadino

This longtime mob boss of Buffalo was one of the original Mafia kingpins to arise out of the establishment of the Commission, the

Mafia governing body. Steven Maggadino ruled upstate New York from the 1930s until his death in July 1974. As a boss, he was often the target of FBI wiretapping.

In 1963, agents heard him voice his dislike of wine in one breath and in another complain about various illnesses he believed resulted from his consumption of cognac. He let it slip that he had a glass of cognac every morning after waking up. Maggadino's underworld associates knew his tastes well. When a fellow mobster from Brooklyn drove up to meet with him around the holidays he brought Maggadino a bottle of cognac for a Christmas present.

Ciro Terranova

Mob nicknames range from the fear-inducing (Scarface, The Blade) to the affectionately descriptive (Lips, The Little Guy). But there was only one "King of the Artichokes." That moniker belonged to Ciro Terranova, an early Mafia figure in New York City. He acquired the name by cornering the market on artichokes, buying them from West Coast suppliers and inflating the price. He pressured grocers in the Italian immigrant neighborhoods to purchase his exorbitantly expensive vegetables, making the "King" a wealthy man. Terranova died in 1938, but had he lived another fourteen years, he would have been able to experience (and no doubt profit from) the launch of the artichoke-infused liqueur known as Cynar.

Cynar does not actually taste like artichokes. It is made from a combination of thirteen herbs and plants, which give it a surprisingly smooth yet complex flavor, with a slightly bitter taste. Campari Group brought Cynar under its corporate umbrella in 1995, putting it alongside its two other Italian aperitifs, Campari and Aperol.

Low in alcohol (33 proof), Cynar is consumed as a digestif aperitif (after-dinner drink). It works equally well as a pre-dinner aperitif. It also lends a degree of complexity to a variety of cocktails and can be used interchangeably with other bitter spirits.

CYN-CYN

The Cyn-Cyn is basically a Negroni, with Cynar replacing Campari. This recipe appears in the book *Boozehound*.

1 oz. Cynar
1 oz. gin
1 oz. sweet vermouth
Dash orange bitters
2 orange wedges, sliced ½-inch thick
Ice

Combine the Cynar, gin, sweet vermouth, and bitters in a cocktail shaker along with a squeeze of juice from one orange wedge. Fill with ice and shake until well chilled, then strain into a cocktail glass. Garnish with the remaining orange wedge.

Vito Giacalone

High-profile Detroit mobster Vito "Billy Jack" Giacalone was constantly under the microscope of local, state, and federal law enforcement. He was known for running bookmaking operations and for

Mugshot of Detroit mobster Vito "Billy Jack" Giacalone. He became a capo in the Detroit crime family, known as the Partnership. Photo credit: Scott Burnstein.

being one of the last men to see Jimmy Hoffa alive before the labor boss disappeared in 1975.

A federal wiretap on the phone of Tony Giacalone, Billy Jack's brother, caught Billy Jack having some flirtatious conversations with an unknown female in 1964.

"How are you, young lady?" he asks her during one call. "How do you feel? What the hell are you doing there all by yourself? You should be coming over here and having a martini with me. Come in and we will have a party. Yeah, come on in and have a martini and about seven or eight of them, though."

Gus Alex

Greek by heritage, Gus Alex rose through the ranks of the Chicago Outfit to become its top political fixer. He was a regular presence in the political hangouts and alderman offices across the Windy City, even extending his influence to the state capital in Springfield, the headquarters of a small Mafia family led by Frank Zito.

In 1962, an FBI informant was present at a discussion between Alex and his girlfriend. Alex bragged about his extensive liquor collection, valued, by his estimate, at over $2 million. The collection, housed at his residence on North Lake Shore Drive, consisted of wine, champagne, and bottles of scotch that were worth, by Alex's estimate, upwards of $25,000 apiece.

SEAGRAM'S VO CANADIAN COOLER

1¼ oz. Seagram's VO whiskey
1 oz. prepared sweet-and-sour mix
1 oz. orange juice
1 oz. Sprite or similar
Add all ingredients into high ball glass with ice.

Russell Bufalino

The coal country of northeastern Pennsylvania was the breeding ground for one of the lesser-known Mafia clans in the US, the Bufalino family. Named after its longtime head, Russell Bufalino, the group had an empire that stretched across the Pennsylvania towns of Pittston, Scranton, and Wilkes-Barre.

Bufalino was particular when it came to food and drink. A waitress at one of his favorite haunts told law enforcement officials that Bufalino "insists on his spaghetti being cooked one pound of spaghetti per three gallons of water." She also told police that Bufalino only drank Dewar's Scotch (spelled Doughers in the FBI report) with a water chaser.

Santo Trafficante Jr., mob boss of Tampa, whose reach extended across Florida and into pre-Castro Cuba. Photo credit: author collection.

Gerry Anguilo

The longtime underboss of the Patriarca crime family in New England, Gerry Anguilo, was caught on wiretap in the

THE SANTO TRAFFICANTE COCKTAIL

Though it doesn't contain the Florida don's favorite scotch, this cocktail from New York-based Prohibition Distillers has a Sunshine State feel to it because of the layered orange flavors.

3 oz. Orange-Infused Bootlegger vodka
1 oz. blood orange puree
1 oz. fresh orange juice
Dash of Campari

Shake the ingredients in a shaker with ice until well blended. Strain into a chilled martini glass and garnish with an orange twist.

early 1960s discussing a dinner meeting with New York mobsters that featured quite a lot of booze. "They start it off with scotch and VO on the table. Then they turn around and put wine for a toast. Then they turn around and put champagne. Then they turn around and put pitchers of beer on the table. Then they turn around and put Italian wine on the table."

Santo Trafficante Jr.

The mob family in Tampa was never as large as its counterparts in the Northeast and Midwest. But despite its small size, the only Florida-based Mafia family controlled a vast swath of the Sunshine State and extended its tentacles into Cuba. Tampa has one of the largest and oldest Cuban-American communities. During Prohibition, these ties between underworld elements in the Cigar City and Cuba brought vast quantities of rum and molasses into the Gulf.

The Tampa family flourished with the ascendancy of Santo Trafficante Sr. in 1940. But it was his son, Santo Jr., who became Florida's most well-known Mafioso. Though quiet and soft spoken by nature, Santo Jr. preferred the swanky nightclubs and lounges of Miami's

Collins Avenue to the Italian and Cuban restaurants of South Tampa and Ybor City.

On December 18, 1964, Trafficante went to the Hillsborough Hotel Barbershop for a haircut and a manicure. He also had a J&B Scotch and water at the hotel's lounge, as he met with Tampa mobster Johnny "Scarface" Rivera to talk about casino opportunities in Puerto Rico.

Salvatore "Red" Italiano

Before Santo Trafficante Jr. took over leadership of the Tampa Mafia, Red Italiano was one of the top wiseguys in town. In addition to running bolita, bookmaking, and other rackets, Italiano owned a beer distributorship, Anthony Distributors. Through Anthony Distributors, Italiano controlled

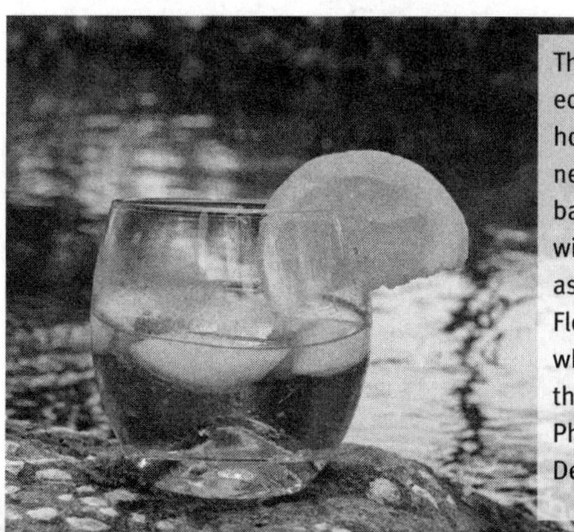

The Red Italiano, equally at home in a dark neighborhood bar where wiseguys gather, as it is next to a Florida swamp where many of them ended up. Photo credit: Sari Deitche.

THE RED ITALIANO

I created the Red Italiano. It merges Campari, signifying Red's Italian heritage, with the southern staple of moonshine (corn-based white whiskey). While it's still possible to get good old-fashioned homemade moonshine in many parts of the South, a host of craft distilleries now turn out high-quality (and high-proof) corn whiskey.

1½ oz. corn whiskey (for a real Florida feel, you can use Bear Gully, made in Winter Haven, Florida)
1 oz. Campari
1 oz. dry vermouth
Dash of orange bitters
Orange slice for garnish

Mix ingredients in mixing glass with ice. Stir for 30 seconds. Strain into glass with ice. Garnish with orange slice.

Miller beer distribution up and down the Gulf Coast of Florida. In 1950, the new underworld regime gave him a choice: leave Tampa or be killed. He lived another twenty years—in Acapulco.

Cutty Sark

Frank Sinatra was dogged for decades by rumors that he associated with mobsters. It's true of course. From his early days in Hoboken, through the Rat Pack years in Vegas, to the latter part of his career, Old Blue Eyes regularly hobnobbed with gangsters. Sinatra seemed as enamored of the "boys" as they were of him. Chicago Outfit mobster Charles Fischetti, Tampa mob boss Santo Trafficante Jr., New Jersey mobster Willie Moretti, and Chicago boss Sam Giancana were just a few of the underworld figures linked to Sinatra over the years.

A vintage Cutty Sark ad. Cutty Sark became a popular whiskey for mobsters. Photo credit: Cutty Sark.

Frank enjoyed cocktails. Though he often abstained from drinking when recording, he always had bottles of his favorite spirits backstage. One of them was Cutty Sark, a blended scotch whiskey popular with wiseguys. Cutty Sark appeared on the 1988 rider for Frank Sinatra's appearance at Bally's in Las Vegas.

Cutty Sark entered the scotch market during the height of Prohibition, becoming a favorite not only of the customers of bootleggers, but of the gangsters themselves, who continued to drink it long after the alcohol trade became legal. This blended scotch was named after the *Cutty Sark*, a British ship built in Scotland in 1869 that was one of the fastest tea clippers ever constructed. Legend has it that Cutty Sark was bootlegged by Captain Bill McCoy, a smuggler based in the Bahamas, the unadulterated contraband giving rise to the phrase "the Real McCoy."

Scott Burnstein has written about wiseguys in books including *Mafia Prince*, which he co-authored with former mobster Phil Leonetti. He observed how for some gangsters Cutty Sark was thicker than blood. "Philadelphia mobster Crazy Phil Leonetti and his uncle, Philly Mafia boss Nicky Scarfo, are both big fans of Cutty Sark and water. . . . Scarfo was famous for drinking that and then when I met his nephew Philip and we went out to eat, that's what he was drinking too—even though they hate each other now and Scarfo has been actively trying to locate and kill his nephew for the last twenty years."

MEMO February 8, 1988

SUBJECT: DRESSING ROOM REQUIREMENTS - FRANK SINATRA

FROM: Richard Sturm

TO: Barry Cregan

There is to be one room service waiter assigned to Mr. Sinatra's Dressing Room nightly. He is to set up the room nightly and remain to make cocktails, or whatever they should request.

DRESSING ROOM SET-UP:

Normal full bar set-up including:

Absolut Vodka	Coke Classic
Cutty Sark	Diet Coke
Jack Daniels	7-Up
Cuervo Gold	Diet 7-Up
Sambuca	Club Soda
Cordon Bleu Cognac	Tonic Water
Corton Charlamagne - 1982	Mixes
Petrus - 1984	Ice

Abundance of Evian Water
Bowl of Assorted Chewing Gum
Hot Water
Coffee
Assorted tea bags
Decaffeinated Lipton Tea Bags
Honey
Cream
Sugar & Sweet & Low
Lemon

NIGHTLY:

Fruit & Cheese & Cracker Tray
Vegetable Tray with dip

Richard Sturm

cc: Al Rapuano
Bob Nickels

LAS VEGAS, NEVADA 89109/702-739-4111

Backstage rider for Frank Sinatra. The Chairman was playing at Bally's on the Vegas Strip in 1988. Photo credit: Phil Samano.

Cutty Sark also had fans on the other side of the law. When a Pennsylvania judge was preparing for a vacation in Florida, he contacted Philadelphia mob boss Angelo Bruno for a favor. He wanted to take eight bottles of Cutty Sark and four bottles of VO for his trip and knew he could get it for free from Bruno.

Some mobsters' wives enjoyed Cutty Sark along with their men. Russell Bufalino, boss of the Northeast Pennsylvania Mafia, was overheard on a wiretap complaining about an underling's wife who seemed to enjoy drinking Cutty Sark with peaches.

Mobster Benjamin "Bugsy" Siegel, Jewish mobster from the Lower East Side in Manhattan, who helped create the modern Las Vegas Strip. Photo credit: Christian Cipollini.

But it was the wiseguys themselves who most embraced the spirit. One of Bufalino's top lieutenants, Angelo Sciandra, drank, according to the local FBI, "moderately, usually preferring Cutty Sark Scotch Whiskey."

Anthony "Tony Jack" Giacalone, a noted Detroit mobster, had a cadre of associates who ran numbers and illegal lottery operations in the inner-city neighborhoods in Detroit. One of those was Harrison "Chink" Brown. Chink was a regular at Club 4800 and patronized a nearby liquor store, where he would spend upwards of $135 a week on Cutty Sark—big money in 1963.

In June of 2007, Rudolph Izzi, a soldier in the New York–based Genovese crime family, was found shot to death at his home in the Bath Beach section of Brooklyn. Izzi, seventy-four at the time of his death, was a true old-school wiseguy who, according to the newspapers, once offered to pay his lawyer with a case of Cutty Sark.

Cutty Sark came under a darker gangland spotlight at the 2009 trial of Gambino crime family member Charles Carneglia. "Crazy Charles," as Carneglia was known to John Gotti Jr., was a prolific hit man, having killed five people, including a high-ranking New York State court officer in 1976. Carneglia's downfall came when his adopted nephew, Kevin McMahon, decided to flip and testify against the gangster. In court, McMahon referred to Carneglia as "a crazed uncle who guzzled bottles of Cutty Sark waiting for calls to commit murder or dissolve corpses in acid at his junkyard."

THE GODFATHER

2 oz. Cutty Sark

1 oz. amaretto

Stir with cubed ice for 20 seconds, strain over fresh cubed ice in a short glass.

BLOOD AND SAND

3 oz. Cutty Sark

¾ oz. sweet vermouth

½ oz. cherry brandy

¾ oz. orange juice

Maraschino cherry for garnish

Combine all ingredients in cocktail shaker with ice. Shake for 10 seconds and strain into cocktail glass. Garnish with the cherry.

Cutty Sark Cocktails

As a lighter blended whiskey, Cutty Sark can be enjoyed straight or on the rocks. But it also makes an excellent ingredient in a variety of cocktails.

A young Meyer Lansky, before he became one of the most significant organized crime figures in history. Photo credit: author collection.

With the popularity of Cutty Sark among the wiseguy set, it's not surprising that one of the cocktails that Cutty Sark promotes is called The Godfather.

The Blood and Sand

The Blood and Sand was created for the 1922 Rudolph Valentino movie of the same name, about an acclaimed Spanish matador. Spirits writer Josh Childs reimagined the cocktail with Cutty Sark.

Meyer Lansky

Despite his nickname, The Little Man, Meyer Lansky is a huge figure in organized crime history. Along with Lucky Luciano, Bugsy Siegel, and Frank Costello, Lansky helped create a new vision of organized crime in America. A Jewish émigré from Poland, Lansky grew up on the Lower East Side of Manhattan with little formal schooling. He quickly attached himself to gangs of Jewish and Italian racketeers who were active in the underworld during Prohibition. By 1931, Lansky and Luciano had made some significant moves against senior Mafia figures in New York (Joe the Boss Masseria

MEYER LANSKY SOUR

This cocktail is found on the menu of the DGS Delicatessen in Washington, DC.

2 oz. gin
1½ oz. Meyer lemon juice
1 dash orange bitters
Simple syrup

Pour all ingredients into a cocktail shaker with ice. Shake for 30 seconds. Strain into chilled glass.

and Salvatore Maranzano). Lansky went on to outlive his compatriots, not only surviving, but surviving in style. He could be seen sporting the latest suits, flawlessly tailored, with a top hat.

According to his daughter, Sandi Lansky, he favored scotch, specifically Dewar's. Scotch was a perennial favorite drink for many gangsters, and Dewar's has long been one of the most popular whiskeys in the United States, especially during the post WWII era. Sandi Lansky said her father "also liked J&B, Cutty Sark, and Smuggler."

Meyer Lansky's name evokes the bygone era of larger-than-life

The Al Capone. With dry vermouth instead of sweet, the Al Capone is drier and lighter than the Boulevardier It's still bitter, like many of Capone's rivals. Photo credit Sari Deitche.

Mug shot of Al Capone, perhaps the most recognized gangster in history. Photo credit: author collection.

AL CAPONE

Saveur magazine printed this recipe, from Brooklyn bartender John Bush. The Al Capone is a close cousin to the Boulevardier.

3 oz. rye whiskey

1½ oz. vermouth

½ oz. Campari

Orange zest to garnish

In a cocktail shaker filled with ice, shake the whiskey, vermouth, and Campari. Strain the mixture into two tumblers, and garnish each with an orange twist.

gangsters—impeccably dressed, smoking a cigar, and running their criminal empire as benevolent dictators. So maybe it's not surprising that it appears in relation to liquor in a number of places with no connection to Lansky. Meyer Lansky's, for example, is the name of a cocktail lounge in Hamburg, Germany. Never mind that the mobster never stepped foot in the lounge, or for that matter, Germany.

BACKROOM MOB

This cocktail mixes elderflower with mint for a mojito-esque flavor.

Mint leaves
½ oz. St-Germain elderflower liquor
½ oz. lime juice
2 oz. bourbon

Muddle mint leaves in cocktail shaker. Add other ingredients with ice in a mixing glass. Stir for 30 seconds. Strain into glass.

Former Chicago Outfit mobster Frank Calabrese Jr. Photo credit: author collection.

Al Capone

Few gangsters loom larger in pop culture than Al Capone. Though he reigned over the Chicago underworld for only a short time, he managed to turn his swagger and media savvy into gangland celebrity. He enjoyed his fame, hobnobbing with politicians, judges, movie stars, singers, stage actors, and baseball players. Capone gained his power during the height of Prohibition. Liquor made his empire and his fortune. It also made him the target of law enforcement and one of the first mob bosses to catch the attention of the federal government.

For his own consumption, Al Capone preferred

Manhattans made with his favorite rye, Templeton. Though he left most of his operation to his underlings, when it came to rye, Capone would get more hands-on. Author Chriss Lyon, a Mafia researcher who specializes in the 1920s, found that, "Even Al Capone realized the promises of Southwestern Michigan, often having his whiskey shipments from Canada stop over at Benton Harbor, Michigan's Hotel Vincent, his headquarters when in town. Capone was said to sample the product before the trucks continued westward on towards Chicago."

THE LUCKY LUCIANO

This drink is an after-dinner cocktail. It's suave and sophisticated, just like Lucky. (Recipe from *Saveur* magazine, April 2014)

1½ oz. Benjamin Prichard's Rye
½ oz. Mancino Vermouth Rosso
½ oz. Mancino Vermouth Secco
¼ tsp. Fernet-Branca
1 Griottines or Luxardo cherry, for garnish

Stir rye, vermouths, and Fernet-Branca in a mixing glass filled with ice; strain into a chilled eggcup or small cocktail glass. Garnish with a cherry.

Frank Calabrese Jr.

Frank Calabrese Jr. was the son of an infamous Chicago hit man. He, along with his brother, Kurt, and uncle, Nick, worked in the family business. But Frank Jr. decided to turn against his father to escape life in the Outfit. In a scheme dubbed Operation Family Secrets, he wore a wire and collected enough information on Outfit bigwigs to allow the FBI to arrest some of the top names in the Chicago Mob. The trial that followed resulted in the conviction of Calabrese Sr. and a number of other mob figures including Joey "The Clown" Lombardo.

LUCKY'S MANHATTAN

In 2011, Basil Hayden's Bourbon worked with HBO to develop signature cocktails inspired by the network's shows. This one references the Luciano character in *Boardwalk Empire*.

1½ parts Basil Hayden's Bourbon
½ part sweet vermouth
½ part dry vermouth
½ part maple syrup
2 dashes of bitters

Stir together bourbon, sweet and dry vermouth, maple syrup, and bitters over ice in a glass. Garnish with a maraschino cherry.

Calabrese Jr. may have turned on his family, but his tastes still reflect his Italian heritage. He favors red wine, "either homemade or Amarone. I like to sip Nonino Grappa also."

Lucky Luciano

As mentioned earlier in this chapter, Lucky Luciano was one of the architects of the modern Mafia. Though his reign in America was cut short by prison and deportation to Italy, Luciano was certainly influential, as much for his style as for his criminal exploits. Luciano was the archetypical 1930s-era gangster and no doubt the inspiration for the way many of those who followed dressed and acted.

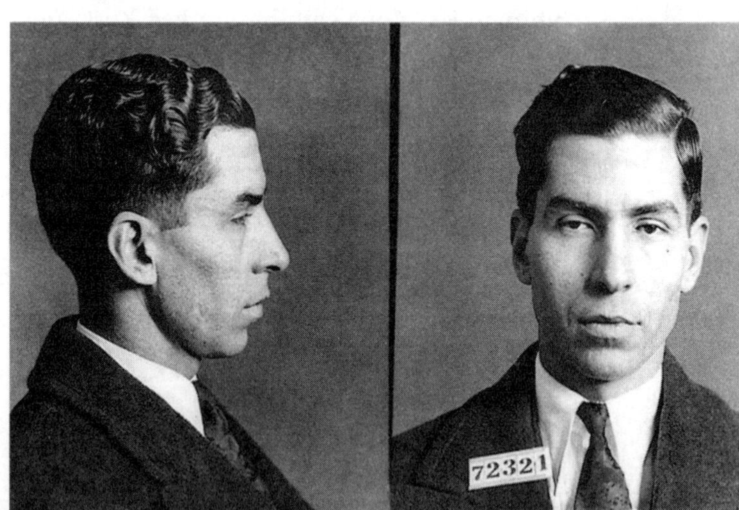

Mug shot of Charlie "Lucky" Luciano. One of the architects of the modern mob, Luciano was heavily targeted by law enforcement and eventually deported to Italy, where he died on January 26, 1962. Photo credit: author collection.

But he was noticeably different from his peers in one way.

"Despite the fact he and his pals made millions off of Prohibition liquor, it seems Charlie was not a particularly 'big' drinker himself," said author Christian Cipollini. Living in exile in Naples, Luciano offered his thoughts on alcohol consumption to a visiting American journalist in 1952. Llewellyn Miller sat down for dinner with the gangster and his girlfriend, Igea Lissoni. After the group enjoyed a meal of fettuccine and calamari, Miller noted that Luciano slowly sipped beer while his girlfriend nursed a glass of wine. Lucky explained the conservative drinking: "People act different sometimes when they're drunk. They bother me."

Though not a big cocktail fan, Lucky has inspired a number of creations over the years.

Vincent Piazza, the actor who played Luciano on *Boardwalk Empire*, grew to

CLASSIC MANHATTAN

2 oz. whiskey
1 oz. sweet vermouth
2–3 dashes Angostura bitters
Maraschino cherry

Add whiskey, vermouth, and dashes of bitters to a mixing glass with ice. Stir for 30 seconds and strain into cocktail glass (most use an upright glass, though I prefer a rocks glass). Add cherry. Repeat.

LITTLE ITALY

This variation of the Manhattan, named for the famous ethnic enclave in Lower Manhattan, swaps out the bitters for Cynar, an artichoke liqueur from Italy that adds bitterness and complexity.

2 oz. whiskey
1 oz. sweet vermouth
½ oz. Cynar
Maraschino cherry

Add whiskey, vermouth, and Cynar to a mixing glass with ice. Stir for 30 seconds and strain into cocktail glass. Add cherry.

YAKUZA COCKTAIL

1 oz. gin
1 oz. dry sake
½ oz. absinthe
½ oz. Maraschino cherry liqueur
½ oz. lime juice
1 dash bitters

Add first five ingredients to cocktail shaker with ice. Shake vigorously and strain into cocktail glass. Add bitters.

love some of the 1930s-era cocktails that his character drank. "I got into Manhattans, just an amazing cocktail. I also tried some quality scotch, like the Macallan, now that is smooth. A couple of standout drinks I've inherited from the show."

The Manhattan

Sometime over the course of the twentieth century, the Manhattan gained a reputation as a wiseguy favorite. The drink was reportedly invented at the Manhattan Club in New York City in 1876, though its origins, like those of many old-school cocktails, are a mix of fact, fiction, and a few too many. William F. Mulhall, a bartender who served drinks in the Grand Saloon of the Hoffman House, a luxurious 300-room hotel located on Broadway, wrote in 1880 that the Manhattan "was invented by a man named Black, who kept a place ten doors below Houston Street on Broadway in the 1860s."

The drink is deceptively simple: rye, sweet vermouth, and bitters (usually in a 2:1:2–3 dashes mix). But it lends itself to many interpretations. Bourbon has replaced rye as the go-to main ingredient, which gives the drink a different flavor profile. Sweet vermouth is usually used, but Lillet or even Cynar can be substituted. Finally, no Manhattan should ever be made without bitters, which round out the drink as no other ingredient can.

The Manhattan's reign as a top gangster drink is likely related to its ubiquity in barrooms and speakeasies during Prohibition, when whiskey and rye were not only among the most popular spirits served, but the most commonly smuggled across the Great Lakes and the Atlantic.

MOLOTOV COCKTAIL

1½ oz. vodka
¼ oz. 151-proof rum
Add vodka to shot glass. Float the rum on top. Light on fire and take the shot.

Yakuza

The largest criminal syndicate in the world is virtually unknown outside of its homeland. The Yakuza control illegal and legal enterprises from their base in Japan, with interests extending across the globe. Sometimes identified by their ornate tattoos, the Yakuza are a syndicate that follows strict rules of decorum and operation. In Japan, they own and operate bars and lounges from Kyoto to Tokyo. The gangsters themselves are fans of scotch and fine whiskeys, especially the Japanese whiskeys that are taking the spirits world by storm. The syndicate's namesake cocktail doesn't feature whiskey. But it does include that most Japanese of spirits, sake.

Molotov Cocktail

Okay, so no discussion of cocktails and gangsters would be complete without the Molotov cocktail, that concoction ubiquitous during Prohibition, labor wars, and mob disputes.

I'm, of course, talking about a shot of vodka with a little high-proof rum on top. Light it with a match and drink it down quickly. It's just what the mobster under pressure needs to take the edge off.

What? Did you think I was talking about a bottle filled with gasoline, lit on fire, and thrown into a rival's business?

CHAPTER 7

Gangster Bars

Wiseguys look for attention. A good mob bar is where they have a book and know everybody.

FORMER GANGSTER JOHN ALITE

The gangster bar is dark and mysterious, with thick clouds of smoke, and just enough light to see where you are going but not enough to make out faces. These establishments range from small corner dives to opulent casinos, from the backroom of a social club to the bar of a famous steakhouse. They are used for socializing and scheming, as a hangout and sometimes as a headquarters. Many mob bars are part of restaurants, affording easy movement from the dining room to the after-hours lounge. Some are hotel and airport bars. While many are in seedy neighborhoods, others are found in country clubs and upscale parts of town. There are private social clubs and biker headquarters for members only (and the occasional visiting mob buff).

Many popular restaurants have served as gathering spots where gangsters parade around their wives and girlfriends, spending lavish sums of money and showing off the fruits of their criminal labor.

Green Chartreuse is the essential ingredient in a Last Word. The spirit is made in France by Carthusian Monks, from a centuries-old recipe using over 130 herbs and plants. Photo credit: Sari Deitche.

Sometimes that has gotten the wiseguys in trouble. In one famous instance, a Bonnano mobster throwing around huge sums of money at a Brooklyn restaurant bar caught the attention of a New York City detective. That cop, Popeye Doyle, began following the spendthrift gangster and stumbled on what became known as the French Connection case.

John Alite, a former Gambino mobster who was at the right hand of John Gotti Jr., described gangster bars in New York. "Wiseguys look for attention. A good mob bar is where they have a hook and know everybody. You got to keep in mind that most wiseguys are cheap. But in the mob bars and clubs, they'll flash money. I've seen guys spend $20,000 to $30,000 a week on martinis and Crystal champagne. They go out three to four nights a week in New York then take the red-eye back and forth to Florida on top of that."

But mob bars and lounges have always been more than a place to hang out and be seen. For many enterprising gangsters—from Irish and Jewish mobsters in the 1920s, through the Mafia in the 1950s and '60s, to the urban gangsters of today—bars and lounges have been a place to launder money made through illegal activities.

DETROIT

Detroit Gangster Bars

When people think of the Mafia, Detroit rarely comes to mind. The Motor City evokes images of automobile plants, Motown, and urban decay. But the underworld in Detroit has a long history, starting with the Purple Gang of Prohibition-era Michigan, and continuing through the early years of the twenty-first century. In the summer of 2014, Jack Tocco passed away. At the time, he was the longest-reigning mob boss in the US, having ascended to the throne of the Detroit Mafia in 1979. Tocco's associates included the Giacalones and Zerillis, names that were associated with one of the great mysteries in American history, the disappearance of Jimmy Hoffa. It's likely that he was felled by the Detroit mob as a favor to the group's Teamster connections and its associates in the New Jersey Mafia. With the construction of the new Giants Stadium in New Jersey, it's now known for sure that, contrary to rumors, Hoffa was not buried in the old one.

LAST WORD

This cocktail was created in 1920 during the advent of Prohibition at the Detroit Athletic Club. As much a speakeasy as an athletic club, the establishment catered to a clientele that included rum-runners and racketeers.

1 oz. gin
1 oz. green chartreuse
1 oz. maraschino cherry liqueur
1 oz. lime juice

Combine all ingredients into a cocktail shaker with ice. Shake vigorously and strain into cocktail glass.

The Anchor Bar

Located in downtown Detroit on Fort Street, the Anchor Bar is a tavern a block away from the Federal Court House and two major newspapers. Now a hangout for journalists and justices, in the 1970s it also served as the headquarters of a mob bookmaking operation controlled by gangsters Charles "Chickie" Sherman and Sol "Good Looking Sollie" Shindell.

DALLAS

Betting drove Dallas's underworld from the 1930s through the '60s. The Texas gambling syndicate included Benny Binion, who would go on to great riches and acclaim as the owner of Binion's Gambling Hall in Las Vegas. Binion spent his early hardscrabble years in the backroom gambling houses of Dallas. During his career he worked with members of the loosely knit Dixie Mafia, as well as a small La Cosa Nostra crime family closely tied to the mob in New Orleans.

Campisi's Egyptian Restaurant

The Egyptian was the first of nine Campisi's restaurants serving traditional Southern Italian food in Texas. Mainly a restaurant, but also a place to get a nice, old-school cocktail or good bottle of wine, the original Egyptian is a throwback to an earlier era.

Founded in 1946, the restaurant became famous for regulars like Dean Martin and Frank Sinatra, and infamous for some of its other patrons. The FBI saw the Egyptian as "a top meeting place of numerous gamblers and associates of top hoodlum Joseph Francis Civello."

Civello was the long-time boss of the Dallas Mafia. The FBI also reported seeing R.D. Matthews, a shadowy gambling figure who appears in many JFK assassination conspiracy theories, and mobsters like Joe Ianni at the Lounge. Perhaps the restaurant's most notorious customer was Jack Ruby, the future assassin of Lee Harvey Oswald.

The Egyptian was operated by brothers Joe and Sam Campisi, who, according to the FBI, ran high-stakes poker games and other illegal gambling and sports betting out of the lounge in the 1960s. Following Joe Civello's death in 1970, Joe Campisi allegedly took over leadership of organized crime in Dallas. Joe was seen meeting with suspected Mafia leaders like Carlos Marcello of New Orleans before his death in 1990.

TREE LINE

2 bing cherries
½ oz. fresh squeezed lemon juice
2 oz. Leopold's Small Batch Whiskey
½ oz. Leopold's Three Pins Alpine Herbal Liqueur
½ oz. simple syrup

Muddle cherries, lemon juice, and simple syrup; add whiskey and Three Pins; add ice and shake. Serve up. Garnish with a round slice of lemon peel (to replicate the Colorado sun). Drink and enjoy!

DENVER

While Denver does not have a name-specific cocktail, the Tree Line was tagged as Colorado's signature drink after its creator—Marnie Ward, a bartender at Denver's Avenue Grill—won a state contest in 2011.

Denver Gangster Bars

Denver's underworld got its start with Black Hand (Italian gangs) extortion in the early 1900s, as waves of immigrants headed out west to Colorado where they set up rackets in towns like Pueblo and Denver.

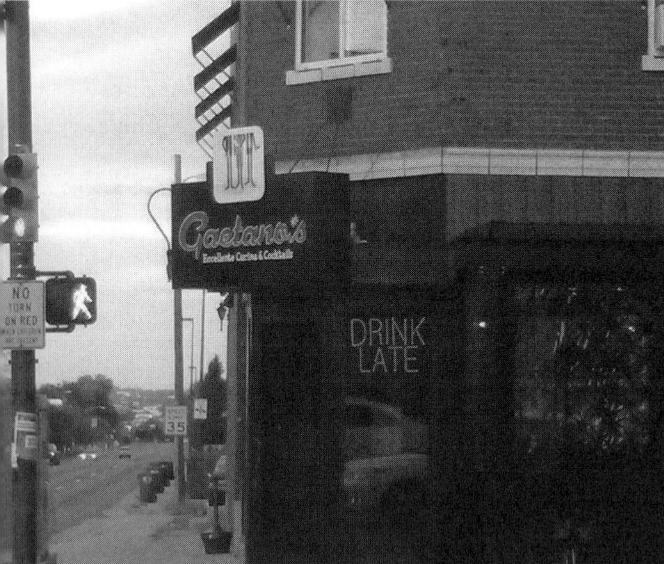

Gaetano's in North Denver was a long-time hangout for the Smaldone brothers, who ran the Denver underworld for most of the twentieth century. Photo credit: author collection.

Gaetano's

Some restaurants downplay their reputation as a former mob hangout, while others just tolerate the occasional mob buff who comes around looking for glimmers of a sordid history. Gaetano's is one of those rare places that celebrate their gangster roots. Gaetano's was, in fact, more than a hangout. It was the headquarters of the Denver Mafia and their monarchy, the Smaldone family.

In contrast to gangsters who flaunted menacing nicknames (Scarface, The Blade, Tough Tony, The Hammer), the Smaldone brothers sported nicknames of a little lower caliber: Chauncey, Flip-Flop, Checkers. But emasculating monikers aside, the Smaldones were serious business. They ran loan-sharking and gambling operations right out of the restaurant, conducting business at the bar, in the booths, or in the basement complete with a tunnel entrance to other parts of North Denver.

Legend has it that in one of the small rooms under the kitchen, Frank Sinatra and Sammy Davis Jr. played craps with some of Denver's most notorious hoodlums. The men's room sports a wall-size replica of a Mafia chart from the Denver police, showing all the major gangsters in town, as well as some of their brethren in Pueblo, Colorado.

Gaetano's also features a modern cocktail bar that takes the classics and puts a spin on them. The cocktail menu is constantly changing and bringing new and edgy drinks to Denver. Still, sitting at the bar sipping one of its craft cocktails, or in a booth eating pasta carbonara, you feel like you've been transported back to the days when the Smaldones held court.

The Cruise Room

Located around the corner from Union Station in downtown Denver, the Oxford Hotel opened in 1891. Bootleggers hung out there during Prohibition and some of the dining rooms still have hidden doors once used to cordon off the speakeasy portion of the hotel from prying law enforcement eyes. The ornate hotel is home to an art deco bar with a red ceiling and walls. The Cruise Room opened the day after Prohibition ended and to this day oozes a 1940s vibe, offering an inventive mix of classic and new cocktails.

If you go there (and you should), ask for Joel Catanzaro. Officially, he's head bartender. Unofficially, he's Oxford Hotel's historian. While he's mixing you an excellent drink, he may also share what he's learned during extensive research into the Oxford's shady past.

The Smaldones, who "ran the underground activities in Pueblo and Denver, used to frequent our speakeasy," said Catanzaro. "The Rose Room, which later became known as 'The Governors Room,' was the speakeasy. The Governor himself during Prohibition would drink in our speakeasy and hence the alternate name the Rose Room was given. There still is a secret door in the Governor's Room and there used to be kick-away panels to hide booze in case they needed to hide it quickly."

The Cruise Room was also part of an underground complex that ran from Union Station to the Oxford Hotel. "In the men's bathroom there is a door where one tunnel would enter. Prostitutes were also brought in through these tunnels," said Catanzaro. "Al Capone was also known to have been in Denver many times in the tunnel system. Capone had a vacation home outside Colorado Springs."

El Paisano

Catanzaro's family originally came from Fiumefreddo di Sicilia, near where scenes for *The Godfather* were filmed (the closest thing they've got to a mob connection). Catanzaro wears his Sicilian heritage proudly, especially when he talks about his late grandfather, Sebastino Lupo Cantanzaro.

"The Cruise Room is my grandpa!" he said. "Swing music and beautiful people. Including beautiful women, which my grandfather always enjoyed flirting and conversing with."

EL PAISANO

2 oz. Bookers Bourbon (126–134 proof)
½ oz. Amaro Averna (Sicilian liqueur)
½ oz. Carpano Antica sweet vermouth
2 dashes Fee Brothers orange bitters.
Stir for 30 seconds. Strain in martini glass. Serve with a blood orange twist (Sicilian-grown fruit)

Joel Catanzaro's favorite cocktail, and one he serves up regularly, is the El Paisano. "I love whiskey and, being a mixologist, I thought of a cocktail that I know I would like and uses some ingredients that are found in Sicilia and have a Mafia theme. After a long day of mob activity I think they would have liked this. *Paison* means 'peasant,' so if any regular Sicilian came into the Cruise Room they would want a bang for their buck."

BOSTON

The Cotton Club

Boston had its own version of the Cotton Club at 888 Tremont Street in Roxbury. Like the famous New York nightclub, it was steeped in jazz and illegal booze during Prohibition. Unlike the New York club, however, Boston's Cotton Club reportedly allowed both whites and blacks. The Cotton Club was owned by Charles "King" Solomon. The Jewish gangster was a successful bootlegger, and also, according to the newspapers, "New England's reputed overlord of vice, liquor, and narcotics." Solomon was killed by rival gangsters in his own club in 1933. The club remained a popular music venue through the early 1980s.

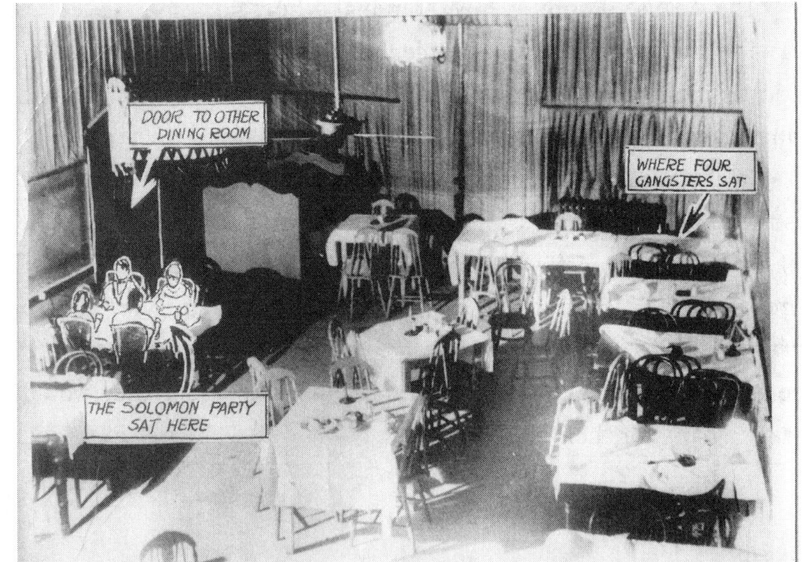

Scene of the 1933 murder of Prohibition kingpin Charles King Solomon. He was killed in Boston's Cotton Club, at 888 Tremont Street in Roxbury. It's currently being renovated into apartments. Photo credit: Christian Cipollini.

The North End

The North End of Boston oozes character, with its historic buildings and web of narrow, winding streets and alleys. Unlike Italian ethnic enclaves in many other cities, the North End maintains its vibrancy, boasting a mix of busy restaurants, bars, and shops.

Café Pompeii

The North End was also home to many noir-ish denizens, including the underboss of the Patriarca crime family, Gennaro Anguilo. One of the most feared mobsters in New England, Anguilo ran his operations out of a small apartment in the North End, on Prince Street, in the 1970s and early '80s. He was often found hanging with his underworld brothers at the Café Pompeii on Hanover Street. The café is still open, though it doesn't serve liquor, only wine and beer. It's better known for its coffee and tea.

SOUTH BOSTON

South Boston, "Southie" to locals (and outsiders who want to sound like a local), is one of the great Irish-American neighborhoods. It was also the base of operations for James "Whitey" Bulger. The Irish mob boss ran the Winter Hill Gang for decades, instilling fear in his enemies and pride in the neighborhood, all the while secretly acting as an informant for the FBI against the Italian Mafia in the North End.

Whitey Bulger fled Boston in 1995, ahead of a massive racketeering indictment. With help from his gangster friends and money he had stashed away around the world, he lived on the lam for sixteen years with his girlfriend, Catherine Greig. They settled in Santa Monica and enjoyed going out (a typical evening: two Grey Goose cocktails for him, two Chardonnays for her). The good times came to an end in June of 2011 when the FBI, acting on a tip, arrested Bulger. He is currently serving two life terms for racketeering and involvement in nineteen murders.

Triple O's Lounge

The Triple O's logo on the building was bookended by logos for Coors Light and Rolling Rock. With windows displaying Budweiser and Killian's Red neon signs, Triple O's looked like the quintessential neighborhood bar.

But Triple O's, located on West Broadway in Southie, was also where Bulger would meet with his underlings to enjoy a beer and plot crimes. One of Bulger's chief lieutenants, Kevin Weeks, who would later turn against his boss, got his start in the Winter Hill Gang as a bar back at Triple O's. One night when a fight was getting out of hand, Weeks came to the bouncer's aid and knocked out a couple of patrons, proving he had at least one of the skills needed to be a wiseguy.

Triple O's became so notorious in South Boston that one columnist nicknamed it the "Bucket of Blood."

South Boston Liquor Mart

Some law-abiding citizens in South Boston looked up to Whitey Bulger as a folk hero. Others feared him as a predator who extorted and worked over residents, leaving them too terrified to go to the police. The Rakeses, a couple who opened a liquor store in Southie, belonged to the second camp. Bulger wanted the store as his new headquarters. One night he visited the husband and threatened him and his children, forcing him to sell the business (then called Stippos) to Bulger and his henchmen. It became the South Boston Liquor Mart, supplying booze to many neighborhood events, including parties held by the local FBI field office.

Jay's Lounge

This lounge at 253 Tremont Street was part of what was known as the "Combat Zone," an area of strip bars, peep shows, and other adult entertainment establishments in a seedy section of Boston in the 1970s. The Mafia, of course, had its hands in on the action. Jay's Lounge, owned by the Anguilo brothers, was a hangout for local wiseguys. The area has now cleaned up and the lounge has been replaced by an Abby Lane Food & Spirits.

KANSAS CITY

Kansas City's claim to fame includes jazz and barbeque, while its claim to infamy includes its local Mafia family, whose operation reached across the Midwest and all the way out to Las Vegas, and political boss Tom Pendergrast, who ruled over Kansas City politics from 1925 through 1939. His reign kept the liquor flowing through Prohibition. Author Frank Hayde is a chronicler of Kansas City crime. In keeping with the pride he has for KC, his favorite beers are from the city's own Boulevard Beer brewery. He prefers Boulevard Irish Ale and KC Pils. In keeping with his interest in crime, he also drinks Boss Tom's Golden Bock, named after Pendergrast.

Berbiglia Wine & Spirits

"As anyone from KC knows, Berbiglia has been the leading name in retail liquor in Kansas City for generations," said Hayde. His book *Italian Gardens: A History of Kansas City Through its Favorite Restaurant* revealed that Kansas City mob figures, the DiGiovani brothers, started Mike Berbiglia in the liquor business in the early part of the twentieth century. "Today, Berbiglia's is still the most ubiquitous chain in the city. Most Kansas City residents driving home from work will pass by a Berbiglia's."

River Market

The River Market neighborhood in Kansas City is filled with shops, businesses, and restaurants. But the respectable image the area cultivates now is shadowed by a violent past. In the 1970s, the area was transformed into River Quay and filled with bars. But a rift in the local underworld led to a war that used the Quay as the battleground. As Frank Hayde noted, "Kansas City is probably the only place where an entire nightclub district was destroyed in a gang war in the 1970s. There were bars like the Virginian Tavern, where the Spero brothers were attacked. Judge Roy Bean's was one of the taverns that blew sky high in an explosion still talked about today."

THE CHICAGO COCKTAIL

This version, featured in *Imbibe*, was adapted from *The Savoy Cocktail Book*.

2 oz. brandy
1 dash Cointreau
1 dash Angostura bitters
Sparkling wine

Tools: mixing glass, bar spoon, strainer

Glass: flute

Garnish: sugared rim

Prepare the glass by rubbing a lemon slice around the rim and dipping it in superfine sugar. Combine the brandy, Cointreau, and bitters in mixing glass with ice. Stir, strain into a glass, and top with sparkling wine.

Other Kansas City Mob Bars

The Famous, 1215 Baltimore Avenue—Mobsters William and Joseph Cammisano owned this bar, which would later be replaced at this address by a Holiday Inn.

The Fortress, 1205 E 85th Street—"It was owned by made man Jimmy Duardi," said Kansas City mob expert Frank Hayde. "The Fortress was the site of some rumbles between Duardi's crew and some members of the Kansas City Chiefs in the 1970s." It's now the site of BB's Lawnside BBQ.

Goldfinger's Living Room Lounge, 3810 Broadway Boulevard—Owned by the brother of underboss Carl DeLuna, it was one of the top mob hangouts in Kansas City. Law-abiding types now go there to get a drink in a place renamed Mini Bar.

Pompeii Room/Bagdad Lounge, 3712 Broadway—The bar that used to be located here was at one time called the Pompeii Room and at another time the Bagdad Lounge. Kansas City mobsters owned it in both incarnations. The Uptown Theater has since been built on the site.

Shady Lady Lounge, 2800 E. 12th Street—This lounge is a strip club located near a used car lot where, according to Frank Hayde, "[mobster] Carl Spero was blown up by a bomb in 1984."

CHICAGO

The Chicago Cocktail

A cocktail with a murky past, The Chicago dates back to the late nineteenth century, though it was made famous in the Windy City through a 1931 tome, *Dining in Chicago* by John Drury, an author with a varied work history (including stints as a Marshall Field's clerk, WWI soldier, police reporter, and book reviewer).

Drury's version of the cocktail (the half-gill is 2 ounces):

"Fill the mixing glass half full of broken ice, add one or two dashes of Angostura Bitters, add three dashes of Curaçao and one-half a gill of Brandy. Stir well, strain into cocktail glass; add an olive or cherry, squeeze a lemon peel and drop it into the glass, and pour a little Champagne on top. Before straining the mixture into the cocktail glass, moisten the outside borders of the glass with lemon juice and dip into pulverized sugar."

Drury adds that, "Robert, of the American Bar at Nice, and formerly of the Embassy Club, London, vouches for the Chicago cocktail—and you'll agree that his vouching is above question."

Chicago Gangster Bars

For gangster mystique, no city beats Chicago, the onetime playground and battlefield of the notorious Al Capone. Despite his short reign as a mob boss, Capone remains an indelible part of American pop culture, his image and name as recognizable today as it was back in 1920s Chicago, where Capone and his men waged war after war for control of the city's rackets, especially illicit alcohol.

Ironically though, Capone was not the head of the mob for very long, nor was he the most powerful Chicago mobster of all time. For sheer longevity and influence, Anthony "Joe Batters" Accardo takes the prize. Accardo was the boss and consigliere for the Chicago Outfit for most of the twentieth century, far outlasting both Capone and another contender for top Chicago hoodlum, Sam "Momo" Giancana.

The Chicago Outfit had an oversized presence in the liquor industry in Chicago, extending to bars and lounges throughout the Chicagoland area. It leveraged political connections to maintain control over liquor licensing and zoning laws. Its allies included men like Pat Marcy, a political boss in the Democratic Party. As an assistant to an alderman in the 1960s, Marcy maintained, according to the feds, "a tight control in effort to improve the business posture of Chicago hoodlums in the operation of bars."

Armand's

Frank Calabrese Jr., son of Chicago mobster Frank Sr., enjoyed Chicago's nightlife and was a regular at the mob bars that dotted Chicago's neighborhoods. "My favorite bar was the lounge in Armands restaurant on Grand Ave in Elmwood Park," he said. "But every Italian neighborhood had a place where everyone hung out. Most of the mob bars are because of location (neighborhood) and knowing the owner."

The Green Mill

Legendary Chicago lounge The Green Mill regularly hosted wiseguys, including Al Capone, during Prohibition. There's a booth, facing the stage on the right-hand side, that the bar's staff still call the Capone booth. The mob boss would sit there and watch the top jazz acts of the day. As long as he stayed in the booth, no one could come in or leave the Mill. Today the lounge attracts artists from poets to jazzmen, who come to perform or just be inspired by the retro booths and chill bar. Current owner David Jemilo proudly plays up the lounge's past.

"It's been there in the same place for over 100 years," he said. "A big portion of Chicago history is the mob and Prohibition. With Al Capone hanging out there, and the fact that Machine Gun McGurn owned it, that makes it special. The Green Mill is official Chicago. I also run it straight, no messing around."

The Green Mill, favorite haunt of Al Capone and Chicago nightclub institution. Photo credit: author collection.

Richard's

Richard's Bar, located at the intersection of W. Grand and W. Milwaukee Avenues, is a true neighborhood dive. The door is painted up as an Italian flag and a huge movie banner of *Goodfellas*, not to mention pics of Al Capone and other famous Chicago gangsters, adorn the walls.

Richard's is not a high-end cocktail lounge, but a place to order a shot of whiskey and a can of Old Style. It's become a night spot for a younger crowd, but for years it was known as a hangout for members of the Chicago Outfit's Grand Avenue crew. And if you do some urban exploring, you can find remnants of the crew that still live and "work" around the neighborhood . . . allegedly. If you're hungry after Richard's, head next door to La Scarola restaurant, longtime hangout for Chicago mob boss Joey "The Clown" Lombardo.

Tommy Gun's Garage

Using Capone-era Chicago as its motif, Tommy Gun's Garage is one of those cheesetastic themed restaurants that invite as much ridicule as good-natured fun. Though the restaurant and floor show are decidedly non-historic, its location at 2114 S. Wabash Street is next to the now-defunct Room 21, housed in an old brewery, which was frequented by Capone and his gang. It took a remodeling project for the current owner of Tommy Gun's Garage to discover the full extent of the restaurant's mob ties.

"When we were doing some work putting the plumbing in for the cappuccino maker, we found something. So Jerry Kleiner, the owner, said 'tear it all down' and we found this passageway," said manager John Nowowiejski. The passageway is believed to have been used by gangsters to escape if police raided the brewery.

Just south of Tommy's on Wabash Street is a large vacant lot that was the site of an establishment run by Big Jim Colissimmo, a mob boss whose death enabled Capone's mentor, Johnny Torrio, to ascend to the ranks of top mobsters in Chicago.

FOX RIVER COCKTAIL

1 sugar cube
5 dashes peach bitters
Ice
2 tsp. crème de cacao
2 oz. whiskey
1 lemon peel

Saturate sugar cube in peach bitters by placing the cube into a rocks glass and pouring enough peach bitters over cube to saturate. Place one large ice cube (or a few smaller ice cubes) in the glass. Pour crème de cacao into the glass, then add whiskey. Squeeze a lemon peel over the top and stir slightly (three to four swirls of the wrist—no bar utensils needed).

More Chicago Bars

The Armory Lounge, 7427 W. Roosevelt Road—The FBI labeled this bar a "known meeting place of Chicago hoodlums."Frequent guests included Chuckie English. (You can see what happened to Chuckie just below, at Horwath's.) The address now belongs to Andrea's Restaurant.

Eddie Foy's Cocktail Lounge, 753 South Wabash Avenue—This bar is purported to have been owned by Al "Pizza Al" Tornabene, an Outfit member who died in 2009.

SAZERAC

1 cube sugar
1½ oz. rye
3 dashes Peychaud's Bitters
¼ oz. absinthe
Lemon peel

Put the sugar cube in a mixing glass and add a little bit of water. Smash the cube. Add the rye, bitters, and ice. Stir. Coat the inside of a cocktail glass with absinthe. Strain the rye mixture into the cocktail glass and garnish with a lemon peel.

The site of illegal liquor raids in 1961, Eddie Foy's closed in 1964. Today at this location is the Papermaker's Garden, a sustainability project for Columbia College.

Horwath's, 1850 N. Harlem Avenue—A speakeasy during Prohibition, this establishment became a top hangout for Outfit members in the 1970s and '80s. It was also where Chuckie English was gunned down in a mob hit in 1985. It closed in the early 2000s. A Staples now stands in its place.

MGM Lounge, 1839 Cicero Avenue—Known as "MGM Nicky's" for the owner, Nicky Kokenas, this bar had a list of regulars that included mobsters Gus Alex, Murray "The Camel" Humphreys, Tony Accardo, and Sam Giancana.

Rosebud, 720 N. Rush Street—Now known as Rosebud on Rush, this bar is part of a popular Chicago restaurant chain. This location and the Rosebud on Taylor have been identified by various law enforcement officials as Outfit hangouts over the years.

Fox River Cocktail

Author, bartender, and restaurateur Matt Seiter became fascinated with this drink after reading about it in 1927's *Barflies and Cocktails*. He researched the origins of the drink and traced it to Fox River

Grove on the banks of the Fox River. The cocktail was likely created at the Crystal Ballroom, a speakeasy owned by Louis Cernocky, a Czech immigrant who quickly became acquainted with the "social influencers" of Chicago and is said to have become a liquor distributor for Capone

The drink is easy to make and, as Seiter notes, "The sugar cube will dissolve as you sip the drink. It is strong at first, but once the ice and sugar melts, it weakens and additional flavors are exposed."

ABSINTHE FRAPPE

This cocktail was created in 1874 at the Old Absinthe House in New Orleans.

6–8 mint leaves
1½ oz. absinthe
½ oz. simple syrup
2 oz. soda water
Crushed ice

Muddle the mint leaves in the bottle of a cocktail shaker. Add the absinthe and simple syrup. Shake vigorously for 30 seconds. Strain into cocktail glass. Add ice and soda water, garnish with a mint leaf.

NEW ORLEANS

While New Orleans does not have a drink named for it, the city is the birthplace of some of the most popular and inventive cocktails in American libation history. In fact, the Museum of the American Cocktail is located in the heart of this iconic drinking town. The city has a similarly rich underworld history, dating back to the late 1800s.

Sazerac

The Sazerac may be the first true American cocktail. In 1838, pharmacist Antoine Amedie Peychaud created the drink in his pharmacy, where he plied his mixology skills after hours. He also developed Peychaud's bitters, an essential ingredient in any good bar to this day.

The Dungeon, New Orleans. Photo credit: author collection.

Supposedly, Peychaud was a fan of a French brandy, Sazerac-de-Forge et fils. In its original recipe, this cocktail had brandy as the main ingredient. In the mid-1800s that was changed to rye, as it stands today.

Absinthe

Popular in the 1800s with writers and artists in Europe, absinthe later found its way to New Orleans, where the French Quarter became a haven for artists fueled by the wormwood liqueur with a sharp licorice flavor. Absinthe was eventually banned in the United States, leaving its availability to the black market. Now, however, the ban has been lifted and high-quality absinthe from Europe, as well as American-made styles, are widely available.

Southern Comfort is a liqueur that originated in New Orleans. Known for its unique blend of fruit and spice flavors, it's a versatile ingredient in a variety of cocktails. The first Southern Comfort drink was created by the inventor of Southern Comfort, Martin Wilkes Heron. The St. Louis cocktail was simply Southern Comfort with some peach juice. Adjust the ratios to make it as strong as you like.

NEW ORLEANS GANGSTER BARS

The 500 Club

Marcello crime family member Frank Caracci (the family got its name from its long-time leader Carlos Marcello), owned this bar at 441 Bourbon Street in the heart of New Orleans. One of a network of bars and nightclubs underworld figures operated in New Orleans, the 500 Club featured strippers into the early 1970s.

Black Magic Bar and Lounge

The French Quarter Visitor Information Center at 100 Royal Street welcomes tourists from around the world. The building that used to be located there welcomed customers from the underworld. The Black Magic Bar and Lounge opened on June 14, 1961. The proprietor, known locally as Sammy Paxton, was actually Salvatore Amarena, a New York-born gangster who ran with the Trafficante family in Tampa and pre-Castro Cuba before becoming an associate of the Marcello family in New Orleans.

MARCELLO'S MANHATTAN

2 oz. Bulleit bourbon
¾ oz. Carpano Antica vermouth
Dash of Angostura bitters
Combine ingredients in a shaker with ice. Stir vigorously for 30 seconds. Strain into cocktail glass.

The Dungeon

Located at 738 Toulouse Street, the (fittingly dark and noirish) Dungeon was originally a private club exclusively for owners of Bourbon Street nightclubs and bars. And in the 1960s and '70s, that meant a lot of wiseguys. Owned by Frank Caracci, The Dungeon boasted an impressive underworld membership that included Carlos Marcello's brother (and future mob boss) Joe Marcello; Nino LoScalzo, son of Tampa mobster Angelo "the Hammer" LoScalzo; and mobster Jerome Conforto.

La Louisiane

La Louisiane is one of New Orlean's oldest bars. The building was constructed in 1837 as a residence. In 1881 it was converted to the La Louisiane Hotel and Restaurant, and became known for its Creole cuisine. In 1954, "Diamond" Jim Moran purchased the restaurant and "decorated the place with extravagant Baccarat chandeliers," according to the restaurant's website. Jim and his brother, Tom, were considered by the FBI as "associates of known hoodlums and gamblers in the New Orleans area." The place was also believed to be partly owned by a far more notorious underworld figure, Carlos Marcello, the boss of the New Orleans Mafia for over thirty years.

Carlos Marcello may or may not have enjoyed a cut of the restaurant, but he definitely liked to bring valued guests and other mob figures there for dinner and drinks. One FBI report follows the New Orleans mobster and his wife to La Louisiane, where they dined with Tampa mob boss Santo Trafficante Jr. in January of 1968.

Nowadays, the La Louisiane revels in its gangster past with the Prohibition-themed 21st Amendment bar. Its cocktail menu includes a drink called Any Last Word, made with lavender gin, yellow chartreuse, maraschino liqueur, and lime juice.

Marcello's Manhattan

Though currently not on the 21st Amendment's cocktail list, the bar did (may still if you ask nicely) feature this libation named after New Orleans's famous Mafia don.

Other Former New Orleans Mob Bars

Cuccia's Yale Bar, 635 St. Charles Avenue—This once was the site of a drinking and gambling joint known to be, according to the FBI, "frequented by prostitutes, low characters, drunks, and bums." It's now a law office. Go figure.

D&A Club, 128 Chartres Street—A Marriott hotel has since opened at this address, which used to belong to a gambling place owned by wiseguy Dutz Murrett. Though Murret was not well known, you've heard of his nephew—Lee Harvey Oswald.

Jazz Corner, 1218 Canal Street—Formerly owned by Carlos Marcello's brother, Pascal, the bar no longer exists. A parking lot sits in its place.

Old Gem Bar, 127 Royal Street—Once the site of numerous bookmaking raids by local cops, today it's the site of the Unique Grocery Store.

Saloon Bar, 227 Bourbon Street—Saloon was one of a network of bars in New Orleans where gamblers placed wagers with the Sam Saia organization, "considered to be one of the biggest horse and

SAN FRANCISCO 1

¾ oz. sloe gin
¾ oz. sweet vermouth
¾ oz. dry vermouth
1 dash orange bitters
1 dash Angostura bitters
1 cherry
Add ingredients to cocktail shaker with ice. Shake vigorously and strain into a cocktail glass. Garnish with a cherry.

SAN FRANCISCO 2

2 oz. vodka
2 oz. orange juice
2 oz. crème de bananes
2 oz. grenadine syrup
Add vodka to a Collins glass with ice. Next add in the juice, then the crème de bananes, and drip the grenadine down the inside of the glass. Garnish with an orange and a strawberry.

sports bookmakers in Louisiana," according to the FBI. Today the building houses Beach on Bourbon, a dance club and sports bar.

CALIFORNIA

San Francisco and Los Angeles had their own Mafia families, but they were smaller than the East Coast and Midwest mobs. Law enforcement agents even called the Los Angeles group the "Mickey Mouse Mafia." But both of these California cities were the settings for many famous noir stories and movies. San Francisco especially has embraced its noir history as part of the city's unique culture.

Many of the West Coast wiseguys originally came from back East and had to adjust to different types of underworld meeting places. Forget bars and neighborhood clubs. As former LA mobster Kenji Gallo observed, "The West Coast is all about the food. We don't have any social clubs out here."

SAN FRANCISCO

A 1967 FBI memo described the San Francisco mob as "small, quiet, and closed to membership." A gangster by the name of James Lanza led this tiny crime family for the latter part of the twentieth century. The San Francisco family came under a rare moment of scrutiny when a 1969 *Life* magazine article alleged that then-mayor Joseph Alioto was connected to organized crime. Alioto responded with a libel suit and won a $450,000 judgment.

The Menlo Club

The Menlo Club, located on Turk Street in San Francisco, served as the hangout and headquarters of gambling kingpin Elmer "Big Bones" Remmer, a reputed associate of East Coast mobsters like Lucky Luciano. The Menlo Club was also frequented by Jack Ruby, Chicago mob associate, nightclub owner, and assassin of Lee Harvey Oswald.

The Town House Bar

This establishment, on Doyle Street in Emeryville, was a hangout for gangsters during Prohibition and into the 1940s for local gamblers like Big Bones Remmer.

San Francisco Cocktail

In 2014, Lauren Sloss wrote in the website *The Bold Italic* about her search for a cocktail that represents the city.

"Well, there is a San Francisco cocktail. Two, actually—one is sloe gin–based, and served up with dry and sweet vermouth, orange and aromatic bitters, and a cherry. The other is vodka-based, and is served over ice with Triple Sec, crème de bananes, fruit juice, and grenadine."

SAN DIEGO

Bernardo Winery

San Francisco mob boss James Lanza's father, Francesco Lanza, "operated the Bernando Winery in Escondido near San Diego with Nick Licata," according to the FBI. Licata was a Los Angeles-based mob figure. The winery was also a favorite of Frank DeSimone, who ruled the Los Angeles Mafia from 1956 until his death in 1967. During one visit to San Diego, DeSimone remarked to a fellow mobster that "he could not find a good meal in San Diego and was going to the Bernardo Winery." Other mobsters who frequented the winery included Joe Adamo and Tony Mirabile.

Lanza and Licata sold the winery in 1934 to Vincent Rizzo. The Bernardo Winery is today still thriving and still owned and operated by the Rizzo family. That's family, not "family."

LOS ANGELES/PALM SPRINGS

Sherry's

Located on the famous Sunset Strip, Sherry's was the site of an attempt on the life of Mickey Cohen in July of 1949. Jack Dragna, head of the Mafia in LA at the time, sent some of his men to ambush Cohen. Sherry's later became the iconic music venue, the Key Club, which closed in 2013.

Mickey Cohen on the Sunset Strip in Los Angeles, at the scene of an attempt on his life. Photo credit: Christian Cipollini.

The Cock N' Bull was at 9170 Sunset Blvd., just a half mile down the Strip from a haberdashery at 8800 Sunset Blvd., the 1940s and '50s headquarters of notorious LA gangster Mickey Cohen.

Chateau Marmont

The luxurious Chateau Marmont at 8221 Sunset Boulevard still draws discerning travelers. In the 1940s and '50s, it attracted the literary set, as well as Los Angeles underworld figures like Mickey Chen and LA Mafia boss Jack Dragna.

The Standard Hollywood Hotel

Located at 8300 Sunset Boulevard, The Standard Hollywood Hotel sits in the heart of West Hollywood. It's a boutique hotel with a neo-retro vibe. But in the 1960s, it was a classic retro hotel run by Eddie Trascher, an associate of Mickey Cohen, who operated it for the Chicago Outfit. Eddie turned the aging, dilapidated hotel into a vibrant scene, making big profits for his partners in the Chicago mob, and for himself, as described in *Balls: The Life of Eddie Trascher, Gentleman Gangster*, which I co-wrote with Ken Sanz. "Eddie began sending Chicago $300 a day. . . Cozzi and his friends were thrilled, but they had no idea that Eddie was keeping a dollar for every dollar he sent them. As long as he kept the books right, they would never know what he was making."

Frankie's on Melrose

From the time it opened in the mid-1980s, many LA wiseguys have hung out at Frankie's on Melrose, a New York-style Italian restaurant that still serves up heaping bowls of pasta and seafood. "Jimmy Caci, Ronnie Lorenzo and Joe Dente from New York would go there. I saw Joe Isgro in there a lot. You'd see actors as well. Joe Pesci was always there," recalled former LA mobster Kenji Gallo.

Club 340

Kenji Gallo used to meet up with Los Angeles (by way of Buffalo) mobster Jimmy Caci at Club 340 in Palm Springs. "I think Colombo mobster Jimmy Green Eyes may have owned part of the restaurant," Gallo said. "We used to go there a lot. Bobby Milano used to sing there and you'd see Keely Smith there with him. A lot of Chicago guys would hang out there. I was there when Louie Caruso had a meeting with Jimmy. I was at the table. Caruso wanted to 'make' John Branco. Jimmy went ballistic because John had ratted on a cop who murdered his daughter's husband in Chicago, making John a rat. Plus John did not have the balls to do the work." Jimmy didn't know it, but Branco was an FBI informant at the time.

OAKLAND

Former vice cop turned writer Brian Thiem spent years chasing bad guys on the streets of Oakland.

"I have a hundred experiences with criminal hangout bars. One that's closest to me is Bosn's Locker at 58th Street and Shattuck Ave," he said. "Bosn's Locker was the favorite hangout of Huey Newton and the Black Panthers in the 1960s. He had dinner there in 1967 before shooting OPD Officer John Frey. In the 1990s, heroin had been replaced by crack cocaine as the most popular street drug and the Bushrod Gang ruled the area surrounded by Bushrod Park, a half block from Bosn's Locker:

> "I was working homicide in 1992 and assigned the case when three people were killed and seven wounded in the bar. It stemmed from a dispute between the Bushrod Gang and another rival drug

Former Las Vegas mayor and lawyer Oscar Goodman. Mayor Goodman made his career representing some of Vegas' more colorful and notorious denizens, including mobsters. Photo credit: Oscar Goodman.

gang after which drug kingpin, Keith 'Green Eyes' Barber, ordered his enforcer, Paul Brown, to shoot the rival. Brown entered the bar on a busy night armed with an assault rifle and wearing a ski mask. He sprayed the table where the rival was sitting and the rest of the bar. He didn't hit his intended target and most of those hit were working people with no ties to the drug trade. The name is now Dorsey's Locker as a result of new ownership."

TOP: Sign for Jubilation nightclub in Las Vegas. The club, owned by Paul Anka, opened in 1978 and stayed open until 1987 when it was renamed the Shark Club. BOTTOM: Interior shot of Jubilation in Las Vegas from 1978. Jubilation was located on Harmon Street near The Signature at the MGM Grand. Photo credit: Phil Samano.

LAS VEGAS

As of 2015, only three pre-1970s casinos remained on the Strip. During the writing of this book, the iconic Riviera, opened in April 1955, was closed. It is to be torn down to make room for an expansion of the Convention Center. Downtown Vegas does offer a number of old casinos (Golden Nugget, Fremont, Four Queens) that have resisted the constant pull of the real estate market. But it's often hard to find pieces of even the recent past, let alone the post-WWII era, when men like casino owner and developer Wilbur Clark and mobsters like Gus Greenbaum and Bugsy Siegel helped make Vegas what it is today.

Newspaper ad for the Copa Lounge in Las Vegas. The Copa was located around the corner from the mobbed-up Stardust casino. Photo credit: Phil Samano.

But for all the glitzy new construction, all the glamour and never-ending desert sun, Vegas is a true noir town. The nightclubs, casinos, backrooms, double crosses, cheaters, con men, swindlers, corrupt cops, and mobsters (past and present) blend together in a unique setting. Even if much of classic Vegas has succumbed to the wrecking ball or strategically placed explosives, a visitor can still find some neighborhood bars and off-Strip locations that embrace the ambience of a shadier Las Vegas.

Oscar Goodman

Oscar Goodman is one of the most recognizable people in Las Vegas. He got his start in the 1970s and became known as a mob lawyer, defending clients such as the widely feared Anthony "Tony the Ant" Spilotro, a Chicago Outfit member who ran the Hole in the Wall gang before his murder by fellow gangsters in 1986. Other mob clients included Philly crime boss Nicky Scarfo and his capo Phil Leonetti, and other Vegas-based mobsters like Frank "Lefty" Rosenthal. Goodman served as mayor of Vegas from 1999 till 2011, when his wife succeeded him.

In 2005, Goodman was asked by a group of schoolchildren what he would bring with him to a desert island. Goodman admitted he'd bring a bottle of Bombay Sapphire Gin. His love of Bombay has a uniquely Vegas backstory. "Bob Martin made the sports betting line. He was the oddsmaker's oddsmaker. I would hang with him at the bars at the Sands or Desert Inn. He was the one who got me into drinking my martinis. I drink my Bombay straight up with no vermouth, very cold, and ask for ice on the side. And I get a jalapeño on top of the ice."

Jubilation

Goodman has many stories of old Vegas, including one where he played peacemaker with a couple of wiseguys. "The bar that Tony Spilotro used to go to was off Paradise road and Harmon. It was a place called Jubilation, and was owned by Paul Anka. Tony had his favorite booth in the restaurant. Nobody except Tony sat there.

"One time Spilotro walked in and Jimmy Chagra was sitting in his booth. Tony came in and said 'get out of my booth.' Chagra called him a midget. Tony got pissed off." Goodman realized the confrontation could have escalated into an all-out mob war. "I called both of them into my office and had them work it out."

Copa Lounge

Goodman's favorite Las Vegas hangout was the Copa Lounge, an Italian restaurant and bar on Convention Center Drive, owned by Al Arakelian. "It was the go-to place after hours. I would get phone calls to get people out of jail and we'd go over there and Al would make us a Caesar salad from scratch, mashing anchovies at the table, some eggs, beef, and mushrooms. I'd get that with a good loaf of Italian bread and my martini. It was heaven. To me, that's how I remember classic Vegas."

Piero's

"Piero's is an old-time place that's still here," Goodman said. "It's always been the place the old-timers go, for drinks and dinner." Piero's is at 355 Convention Center Drive.

Dino's

Dino's Lounge is located on the North Strip, south of the Stratosphere, but north of the main group of modern Strip casino resorts. Promoted as the "Last Neighborhood Bar in Las Vegas," it has become an institution over the decades. Dino's opened in 1962, but before that the bar was known as Eddie Trascher's Ringside Liquor Store. Eddie was a gambler and con man who worked as a dealer in many of the old casinos in Vegas, and stole chips by the hundreds

THE 21ST HOUR

Barspoon of acid phosphate
1 oz. sweet vermouth
1 oz. gin
1 oz. yellow chartreuse
3 drops apple bitters
Stir ingredients and strain over ice. Garnish with a cinnamon stick.

each night. He later became a bookmaker with ties to the Mafia in Chicago and Los Angeles, and eventually ended up as an informant for Florida law enforcement against the Trafficante crime family.

When it was the Ringside, the bar attracted gamblers and underworld figures, but also casino employees, especially those from the nearby Riviera, where Eddie was a dealer and stole thousands of dollars in casino chips. The management at the Riviera made it clear what they thought of the Ringside. Posted in all the backrooms and employee lounges was a sign: *Anyone caught entering or exiting a place of business known as Eddie Trascher's Ringside Liquor Store will be automatically terminated from this hotel.*

It's too late to visit the Riviera, but Dino's is still around and should be on any cocktail, or mob, fan's list of must-see places in Vegas.

Frankie's Tiki Room

Located just a few blocks from downtown on West Charleston Boulevard, Frankie's is my favorite bar in Las Vegas. It's not a bar with gangster connections, but for fans of cocktails, particularly those of the tropical variety, it is as close to an old-school tiki lounge as you can find. Expertly crafted tiki cocktails are served in tiki-head glasses, with plenty of fruit and paper umbrellas. The bar itself has a definite noir feel. It's dark and immersive, all the corners decked out in a retro Polynesian theme, and a jukebox plays old surf rock classics.

The Mob Museum

Situated in downtown Las Vegas, the Mob Museum opened on February 14, 2012, the date chosen not to mark the holiday celebrating love, but rather the 1927 St. Valentine's Day Massacre in Chicago. The museum doesn't glorify gangsters, but tells the story of their rise in America and of the law enforcement agents who helped bring the mob down and still work in the fight against organized crime.

That the museum is located in Vegas is important; it reflects the city's mob-soaked past as well as its contrarian, independent spirit. Among the annual events the Museum holds is Repeal Day, to celebrate the end of Prohibition. As part of the festivities, the Museum hosts a bartending competition that brings out Vegas' best mixologists.

The first winner of the Museum's Repeal Day bartending competition was Keith Baker, who has worked at a number of top Vegas bars.

"My winning drink is called The 21st Hour. The name is based on the cocktail party theme of hosting repeal day parties at 9 o'clock, or the 21st hour, in honor of the 21st Amendment," Baker said. "The gin, vermouth, and bitters are all homemade to get the taste I was looking for. The gin is 'bathtub gin' in the sense that I took a neutral spirit (in this case Tito's Vodka) and macerated it in juniper and other flavors, which is a practice that was being used during prohibition. It would have been juniper extract in those days to save on time and money, and because quality wasn't an issue."

A note on acid phosphate, a favorite ingredient of Baker's: "It was used by soda jerks to put citrus in flavored sodas without using flavored citrus juices like lime or lemon. That, along with others such as lactates, are bringing chemistry to bartending in an old-school style and allowing for some interesting possibilities. I hope these become more widely available and cheaper in the future." You can now find acid phosphate online from a number of sources, including Amazon. An 8-oz. bottle is about $20.

BUFFALO

Romanello's Roseland

The iconic Roseland restaurant and bar in Buffalo operated from 1928 until 2005. One night stands out above all the others, as author Nicholas Denmon, who writes novels based on Buffalo organized crime, explained.

"The Romanello family has owned businesses in the area for over eighty-five years, but this particular establishment saw a mafia hit go down right in front of it May 8, 1974. John Cammilleri was walking into the restaurant after being denied a request for greater family 'recognition.' He stormed out and went to Roseland's, where someone yelled his name as he was walking inside. When he turned around he was shot multiple times in the chest and face. He died on the ground in front of the restaurant."

NEW YORK CITY

No surprise, New York City has more gangster hangouts than any other city in America. It is, after all, the national epicenter of the mob. From the tip of Lower Manhattan through all five boroughs, corner bars and dimly lit lounges have served as meeting places and headquarters for New York's gangsters from the early 1900s up to the twenty-first century.

Mob places have ranged from underground gambling clubs in Manhattan's Chinatown and Little Italy to neighborhood red-sauce establishments in East Harlem and Brooklyn. There were social clubs that lined the streets in the Italian, Irish, and African-American neighborhoods, many of which had small bars in them. And during Prohibition it was estimated that over 30,000 speakeasies existed across the city.

Every mobster had his own neighborhood favorites. "When I grew up there were many 'mob bars' in Brooklyn," said former gangster Sonny Girard. "Cocoa Poodle was the one I hung out at when I was really young, then Austin Lounge in Queens, then mostly in places in uptown Manhattan where I would build relationships with legitimate upper-income people."

John Gotti Jr. and his young crew, including John Alite, tore up Manhattan, Queens, and Long Island in the 1990s. Gotti crew member John Alite recalled their hangouts: "We'd go to Regimes, Club A, Stringfellows in Manhattan, Café Iguana, and the Harbor Club—John had a piece of that. Elephis on Northern Boulevard, Queens was a favorite. We'd go to Metro 700 and Channel 80 on Long Island. Guys would pull up with cigarette boats with all the flash and get attention."

Kenji Gallo frequented bars with the Colombo family. "We'd hang out at Aria's on Third Ave. in Brooklyn. It was right down the street from the Blue Zoo Lounge, where we used to have meetings as well. The Blue Zoo was a college bar—really hip, so not the place you'd associate with wiseguys. We would hang out with Allie Shades Persico at the Turquoise in Bay Ridge. That place was a total guido bar. Lots of old wiseguys and young girls. It was also a big hangout for Gambino guys."

When undercover FBI agent Jack Garcia was masquerading as Jack Falcone and infiltrating the Gambino crime family in the early 2000s, he and the guys "hung out a lot at Pasta PaVoi in Port Chester. It was owned by Joe Fornino. Cops from Port Chester Police

Department also hung out at the bar. It was such a well-known gangland hangout that the FBI had the place all wired up."

Copacabana

The Copacabana, one of the best-known nightclubs in New York history, drew a diverse crowd from its opening in 1940 through the mid-1970s. Politicians rubbed elbows with sports figures, while dancers, singers, and mobsters shared drinks and swapped stories. The entertainment was legendary, and the Copa was a favorite spot of Frank Sinatra.

Writer Alex Hortis described a typical night at the Copacabana in his book *The Mob and the City*. "Anthony 'Tony Pro' Provenzano and Anthony 'Fat Tony' Salerno kept a regular table with boxing mobsters Frankie Carbo and Frank Palermo. In they'd strut with silk suits, ridiculing waiters, then making it up with big tips."

Sandi Lansky, daughter of Meyer Lansky, spent a lot of time at the nightclub. "The Copa was wonderful. If you tipped well, you got the good tables. I met Ella Fitzgerald there. She was such a down-to-earth lady. I also went to the El Morocco, and the 21 club, but I liked The Copa. And since most of the big mobsters went there, my dad knew every time I was at the Copa. He'd always ask 'Why aren't you home? You're always out cabareting.'"

The Copacabana has moved locations over the years, closing and reopening. Its current home is at 268 West 47th Street.

The Dearly Departed

Much like Las Vegas, New York City is always in a state of churn. Residents move in and out, businesses come and go, often falling victim to changing real estate markets. Collecting rent from a neighborhood Irish bar is not as lucrative for a landlord as converting the space to a Duane Reade or the ground floor of a luxury condo development. In Manhattan, especially, many famous gangland nightclubs and bars have been lost to gentrification. Some social clubs in Brooklyn still survive, but they also are disappearing as neighborhoods change.

In the past, some of the most lavish nightclubs in Manhattan were also top gangland spots. Many mobsters enjoyed the club scene, as well as the live music. These were the places to be seen, where an enterprising gangland figure could splurge, tossing out hundred-dollar bills to the waiters, maître d's, cocktail waitresses, and bartenders. Even though the mob was supposed to be an underground, secret society, whose members eschewed publicity and shied away from the limelight, in reality most wiseguys loved showing off, whether it was clothes, women, cars, boats, or the giant wads of cash they kept in their pockets.

Jilly's

Jilly's Saloon, at 256 West 52nd Street, was owned and operated by Jilly Rizzo, a close friend and confidant of Frank Sinatra. A regular spot on the underworld circuit in the 1960s and early '70s, it attracted mob figures from Joe Colombo to John Gotti.

The club went into foreclosure in the mid-1970s, but was reopened on September 15, 1977 under the management of Tony DelVecchio, who recounted the night in his book, *Sinatra, Gotti, and Me*. "The place looked great. We had a staff that was on top of things. Naturally, Sinatra was there. So were John Gotti and Junior Persico." Gotti would go on to lead the Gambino crime family and Persico would become the boss of the Colombo family.

HARLEM MUGGER

½ oz. gin
½ oz. vodka
½ oz. light rum
½ oz. tequila
2 oz. champagne
1 oz. cranberry juice
Add ingredients in order listed over a highball glass with ice. Stir till blended. Garnish with a lime wedge.

Hotel Claridge

This hotel, torn down in 1972, was the 1930s headquarters of Lucky Luciano, Bugsy Siegel, Frank Costello, and Meyer Lansky. The foursome got their start in organized crime at this speakeasy, which also attracted thirsty judges and politicians.

The Cotton Club

The Cotton Club, at the corner of Lenox Avenue and 125th Street in Harlem, was best known as a top jazz establishment whose house band was fronted by Duke Ellington. Other performers included the biggest names in jazz history, including Cab Calloway, Fats Waller,

Count Basie, Louis Armstrong, Billie Holiday, Lena Horne, and Ethel Waters.

Boxer Jack Johnson opened the club (then called Club Deluxe) in the early 1920s. Notorious mobster Owney "The Killer" Madden bought it in 1923 and christened it The Cotton Club. Born in England, Madden had emigrated to New York City and joined the Gophers, one of many loosely organized street gangs that flourished around the turn of the twentieth century. He bought the Cotton Club just after being released from prison, where he'd served a nine-year sentence for murder.

Despite its Harlem address, the Cotton Club welcomed whites only (except, of course, for the entertainers). Racial segregation was part of the club's appeal to the white clientele, which included both the upper crust of Manhattan and underworld figures. This mingling of the two worlds proved lucrative for Madden, who took in millions from the establishment. The Harlem location closed in 1935 and the club moved to Midtown in 1936, finally shutting its doors in 1940.

The Stork Club

Madden also had a stake in another venerable New York City night spot, the Stork Club, which Walter Winchell once called "New York's New Yorkiest" club. According to law enforcement reports, Owney Madden "financially backed Sherman Billingsley in the Stork Club."

Billingsley was a reputed Oklahoma bootlegger who started running booze throughout the Midwest with his brother Fred (Fred also worked with Detroit organized crime figures). Billingsley was arrested for bootlegging, and after serving fifteen months in prison relocated to New York City. In 1929, with two of his Oklahoma gambling compatriots, Sherman opened The Stork Club.

Asked about the club's name, Billingsley took the fifth: "Don't ask me how or why I picked the name, because I just don't remember." Among his infamous employees was Vito Genovese, who worked for Billingsley before he became boss of his own crime family. As business grew, Billingsley moved the club to 53rd Street and Fifth Avenue, where it stood from 1934 until it closed in 1965.

GANGSTER BARS STILL STANDING

Neir's

Neir's on 78th Street in Queens is the oldest bar in New York City. It was founded back in 1829 as the Old Blue Pump House. McSorley's in the East Village is often called the oldest bar in New York City, because Woodside, Queens, where Neir's is located, was not part of New York City in the mid-1800s. Regardless, Neir's is an institution. The interior was the setting for several key scenes in *Goodfellas*, including the one where Robert DeNiro dresses down his crew for spending lavishly on cars and furs after the high-profile Lufthansa heist of 1978.

Rao's

Located in the former Italian enclave of East Harlem, Rao's is known for many things, chief among them how nearly impossible it is to get a reservation. Owned by actor Frank Pellegrino, the New York eatery hosts politicians and influencers, singers and authors, DeNiro and Pacino. It also attracts its fair share of wiseguys. On December 22, 2003, Pellegrino asked Broadway actress Rena Strober to sing a song. As she crooned "Don't Rain on My Parade," Lucchese mobster Albert Circelli, seated at the bar, made a comment that she stunk. Fellow gangster Louie Bump-Bump Barone shushed him. After the two exchanged more words Barone pulled out a .38 and shot Circelli dead in front of a packed dinner crowd.

Sparks Steak House

Sparks is the place for a fantastic steak dinner, excellent classic cocktails, and extensive wine list. But for all its culinary attributes, Sparks will forever be known as the place where John Gotti Jr. and his crew gunned down Gambino boss Paul Castellano in December of 1985 right outside the front door.

Old Town Bar

The Old Town Bar at 45 East 18th Street is a throwback to the Tammany Hall days in New York. The bar retains much of its late nineteenth-century charm, along with Prohibition-era updates like hidden compartments to hold alcohol.

Mulberry Street Bar

Located in the heart of what remains of Little Italy, the Mulberry Street Bar has been serving since 1908. Through the years, the bar has been a hangout for many local wiseguys, though few remain to walk the streets of Little Italy anymore. It has also been featured in classic gangster movies like *State of Grace*, *Donnie Brasco*, and *The Godfather III*.

Mr. Bigs Bar and Grill

This bar, located at 596 Tenth Avenue in Hell's Kitchen, was known in the 1970s as the 596 Club. Owned by Jimmy Coonan, leader of the Westies, the Irish mob of Hells Kitchen, the club did not cater to tourists or other outsiders. The dark and dingy dive bar was where loan shark Ruby Stein was killed and dismembered by the Westies. Some neighborhood stories tell of gangsters rolling his head down the length of the bar after they chopped it off. Though the neighborhood has long been cleared of the Westies, the stories, and some say ghosts, remain at the bar.

The Back Room

Located on the Lower East Side, at 102 Norfolk, the Back Room is a true speakeasy. You need a password, after walking down a bare brick hallway, to get inside. The bar retains a 1930s feel, having changed little since the days when Bugsy Siegel, Meyer Lansky, and Lucky Luciano frequented the Back Room, ostensibly for business purposes, but also for the top-flight entertainment. Today, even non-wiseguys can go there to enjoy live jazz and a full suite of classic cocktails.

The Landmark Tavern

Another Hell's Kitchen bar with a gangster past, the Landmark, at 626 Eleventh Avenue opened in 1868 and stayed open as a speakeasy during Prohibition. It was famously the favorite watering hole of actor George Raft, best known for his many gangster roles on screen (most notably as Spats Colombo in *Some Like It Hot*). In real life, Raft was in deep with gangsters, especially in pre-Castro Cuba, where he allegedly owned pieces of casinos with mob figures like Meyer Lansky and Santo Trafficante Jr.

SPRINGFIELD, MASSACHUSETTS

Springfield, Massachusetts might be the last place you'd expect to find an active Mafia family, but for over sixty years it's served as the home of a branch of the NY-based Genovese crime family. The family was relatively low-key until the spectacular November 2003 murder of local crime boss Adolo Bruno. The ensuing indictments crushed most of the remaining mob activity in town.

Monte Carlo

Located in West Springfield, the Monte Carlo opened in 1934. Once owned and operated by the Pugliano family, this Italian eatery has a mob history. Second-generation owner Louis "Louie Pugs" Pugliano and his brother, Frankie Pugs, were reputed associates of the New England-based Patriarca crime family. The Pugliano brothers participated in the assassination of Patriarca powerhouse Mickey Grasso in 1989, one of the tumbling dominoes that led to a major Mafia war in New England. Pugliano spent sixteen years in prison before his release in 2006.

MILWAUKEE, WISCONSIN

Milwaukee, Wisconsin is synonymous with beer, and was once home to some of the largest breweries in the United States, including Schlitz, Miller, and Pabst (only Miller remains). With the explosion of craft and microbreweries in the last decade, Milwaukee again finds itself a hub for beer lovers. Many of the favorite beer halls and watering holes of the city's blue-collar past were also gangland hangouts.

In Milwaukee, the mob was in the beer business pre-, during, and post-Prohibition. "Obviously the street crews weren't pushing barrels of beer on the level of Miller, Pabst, Blatz, Schlitz . . . who can compete with that?" said Milwaukee Mafia expert and author Gavin Schmitt. "But they had their share of liquor hijackings, bootlegging, and getting 'hot' booze into their numerous taverns. The only thing more profitable than selling stolen alcohol wholesale is keeping it and selling it yourself."

Schmitt said there were more than a few mob bars in Milwaukee. "Almost everyone connected to the Milwaukee Family owned or worked at a tavern. The Scene, Ad Lib, Kings IV, Brass Rail, Iron Horse, Casino Bar, Fazio's, Clock Bar, Jack and Vickey's, Alfie's, One Plus One, Mr. Mackey's, Gallaghers, Libby's, Peacock Lounge, the New Yorker, Club Midnite, 808 Club, Riviera, The Pub, etc. etc. Commonly they were found around 3rd, 4th, and Water Streets, but a tavern is never a bad investment in Milwaukee so they could pop up anywhere and were a great place to push 'hot' booze and meat."

The Downtowner

In the early 1960s, Milwaukee mob boss Frank Balistrieri was charged with running B-girls out of the Downtowner to encourage patrons to drink more—and more expensive—booze. After successfully getting himself extricated from the charges, he remarked, "Now they'll know that I can take care of anything."

Scott Burnstein described the bar as "just about as 'downtown' as you can get. Today, that area is a parking ramp for the library, museum, Pabst Theater, etc. The whole time it was there it was owned by Balistrieri, with Rudolph Porchetta managing. It wasn't a 'hidden interest'—everyone knew it was Balistrieri's club. I don't know its exact years of operation. At least as early as 1963, and up through the rest of the decade. By the 1970s, he seemed more focused on his other clubs—the Scene, Ad Lib, Brass Rail, Kings IV. It was probably a hangout, but not as much as the others, especially the Scene and Ad Lib. It's hard to say when it's such a small family . . . do two or three guys hanging out there count as a hangout?"

WASHINGTON, DC

Gangsters operated in Washington, DC. Cue the jokes.

Mockingbird Hill

Derek Brown opened this sherry bar at 1843 7th Street NW, an address with a scandalous past. The website Ghosts of DC researched the location's history, dating back to an illegal gambling raid on a house that stood there in 1928. Ten years later, the site was Howard Social Club, another gambling hall and the place where amateur prizefighter Joshua Collins was stabbed to death after trying to pass off a counterfeit $5 bill.

World Wine and Spirits

Located at 153 Pennsylvania Avenue (about four miles from the White House), World Wine is a typical neighborhood liquor store. But it sits on the site of The Amber Club, a gangland bar and lounge once owned by Joe Nesline, the gambling kingpin of DC. Nesline operated dice games at The Amber in the early 1960s. Before law enforcement pressure closed them down, Nesline continued his gambling activities in DC, as well as in Miami, where he aligned himself with mob figures like the powerful Charlie "the Blade" Tourine.

FLORIDA

Florida has always been, as it is now, a great place for Northerners to vacation and eventually retire. For members of the underworld, it was no different. In the early part of the twentieth century, the state was divided into three parts in terms of organized crime influence. On the West Coast, the Trafficante crime family became the dominant organized crime syndicate, while the more rural central counties were under the control of Harlan Blackburn and his cracker mob. South Florida was open territory. Starting in the 1930s with Al Capone, South Florida became a resting stop for mobsters weary of law enforcement pressure, and the weather, up North. But by the 1960s, many gangland figures were spending long stretches of time in Miami and Fort Lauderdale, running gambling operations, corrupting public officials, and drinking copious amounts of alcohol at the numerous bars, lounges, and nightclubs.

BOCA RATON

Merlino's

Throughout this chapter, I've written about gangster bars that have closed, and ones that still stand but are no longer hangouts for mobsters. Merlino's status is different. It's a new addition to the South Florida dining scene and has garnered some good reviews for its food and cocktail menu. But its real hook is the owner and frequent presence in the dining room greeting guests, Skinny Joey Merlino, former (or, according to the FBI, current) boss of the Philadelphia mob. Skinny Joey participated in a gang war in South Philly between various factions of the crime family. He was convicted of racketeering and upon his release from prison in 2011 relocated to Boca. As of this writing, Skinny Joey had recently finished up a four-month stint in the joint for violating his probation by meeting with fellow mobsters at a South Florida cigar bar.

MIAMI

Vincent Capra's

Vincent Capra's at 8400 Biscayne Boulevard was known as Frank Sinatra's favorite Miami restaurant. According to the *Palm Beach Post*, if Sinatra couldn't make it to the restaurant personally, Capra's "would send some Italian food to his penthouse (at the Fontainebleau)."

Capra's was owned by Vincent Bruno, a close friend of Tampa mob boss Santo Trafficante Jr. (who lived in Miami throughout most of the 1960s and '70s). Trafficante's lawyer, Frank Ragano, recalled, "Anybody who was anybody went to Capra's, from the mayor to movie stars. When Santo walked in, everyone came up to him."

Eden Roc

The Eden Roc is a luxurious hotel located on Collins Avenue in Miami Beach. The hotel was designed by famed architect Morris Lapidus and opened in 1956, right in time for the first heyday of Miami Beach's nightlife. The Eden Roc also became a fashionable place for wiseguys to congregate—and sometimes a little more. According to one FBI report, "Local police in 1961 raided this hotel to break up a $30,000 a week bookmaking operation. Open gambling was permitted by the management last winter season."

On its gangster guest list: Chicago Outfit members Gus Alex, Phil Alderisio, and Sam Giancana; New York mobsters including Carlo Gambino; Philadelphia crime boss Angelo Bruno; Santo Trafficante Jr. and Meyer Lansky.

Fontainebleau

From the time of its construction in 1957, the hotel has been associated with the underworld. Racketeer Max Eder extracted a pay-off to ensure the union didn't strike during the construction. According to the FBI, Eder also saw that mobsters received "the proper cut from gambling, bookmaking, and shylocking at this hotel." Hosting entertainers, politicians, and other celebrities, the Fontainebleau became known, as it still is, as a place to be seen.

Tahiti Bar

The Tahiti Bar and Package Store, located at 244 23rd Street, was one of many tiki-themed bars and lounges that dotted the Miami Beach and North Bay Village nightclub scene, post-WWII at the height of the tiki craze. David Yaras, a particularly notorious Chicago gangster, owned and operated the Tahiti Bar from the 1950s into the early '70s. Ohio-based racketeer Romeo James Civetti had a second career as one of Yaras's chief bartenders. The Tahiti Bar was located next door to Sonny's Restaurant, owned by Joseph "Chickie" Chierico, a well-known "hoodlum" according to Miami PD. Wiseguys hungry after planning crimes at the Tahiti would drop by Sonny's for a bite to eat.

As stated so eloquently by the webmaster of Humuhumu's Critiki website, a veritable cornucopia of tiki bar information, "I'm not clear on exactly what 'Tahiti Package Store' was, but since members of 'the family' were involved in running the Tahiti Bar, I supposed the packages could have been just about anything."

North Bay Village

The small community of North Bay Village sits between Miami Beach and the mainland. A May 1968 grand jury report on the bar district in North Bay Village described how "known hoodlums, jewel thieves, and unsavory characters of all types have been allowed to frequent these bars and restaurants with little or no interference or discouragement from the North Bay Village Police Department, or the managers and owners of these establishments." At that time in the late 1960s, over a hundred mobsters lived in and around the Village and made the rounds of the late-night lounges and nightclubs.

Other Miami Mob Hangouts

Admiral Vee Hotel Lounge, 8000 Biscayne Boulevard—The hotel and adjacent lounge were, according to the FBI, a "hangout for petty thieves, racketeers, and gamblers." There's a film studio there now.

Bonfire Restaurant and Lounge, 79th Street Causeway—Operated by "Radio" Sam Weiner, a racketeer connected to Meyer Lansky, the Bonfire was known for its barbeque and the drinks in its Pinto Lounge. It's no longer there.

Gallagher's, 12605 Biscayne Boulevard—This steak house and lounge was a favorite of the Chicago Outfit, especially Jackie Cerone. Its owner, Joe Lipsky, was allegedly connected to mobster Frank Costello.

Joe Sonken's Gold Coast Lounge, 606 N. Ocean Drive, Hollywood—A few towns up from Miami, the Gold Coast Lounge was opened in 1948 by Chicagoan Joe Sonken, an underworld associate. In its heyday the place to be seen for gangsters from Meyer Lansky to Angelo Bruno to John Gotti, the Lounge closed in 1994 and was purchased by restaurateur Gus Boulis. In 2001, Boulis died in a spectacular gangland hit in Miami, killed by Gambino crime family associates hired by Boulis's disgruntled former business partner. The former Lounge site is now GG's Waterfront Bar and Grill.

Peppermint Twist Lounge, South Dixie Highway. Racketeers Morris Levy and Joe Biele operated this lounge, modeling it after Biele's establishment of the same name in New York City. The New York club was an important landmark in rock 'n' roll history, as the place where The Twist dance craze originated in 1961.

TAMPA

The state's only home-grown mob family had its headquarters in this West Coast Florida city. The syndicate in Tampa grew out of early Anglo, Cuban, and Sicilian gangs that fought for control of bolita (an illegal lottery game) and other rackets in the city. Charlie Wall, known as the Dean of the Underworld, was usurped from his gangland throne in 1940 and Tampa's organized crime came under control of the Mafia, led by Santo Trafficante Sr. When the elder don handed the reins over to his son and namesake, Santo Jr., the Tampa mob expanded its operations throughout Florida and into pre-Castro Cuba.

Interior of the Castaways Lounge in Tampa, circa 1970s. The Castaways was the headquarters of mob underboss Frank "Daddy Frank" Diecidue. Photo credit: author collection.

Castaways

Now known as Lazzara Family Liquors, the Castaways, located on Kennedy Boulevard, served as headquarters for Frank "Daddy Frank" Diecidue, the longtime underboss of the Tampa mob. In the 1970s, he used the Castaways as the base of operations for his crew of arsonists, bookmakers, and hit men.

A current photo of the old Dream Bar in Tampa on Nebraska Avenue. The Dream Bar was owned by the Trafficante family. Mobsters Fano Traficante and Nick Scaglione served as both bartenders and bookmakers for the lounge. Photo credit: Bill Iler.

Dream Bar

The Dream Bar, 2801 Nebraska Avenue, was owned and operated by the Trafficante family. Prominent mobsters who worked at the Dream Bar included Nick Scaglione, as well known for his bookmaking and gambling operations as he was for his bartending skills.

The Columbia Restaurant

One of the oldest restaurants in Florida, the Columbia serves Spanish and Cuban food. Famed for its "1905 salad," The Columbia has an ornate barroom with a well thought-out cocktail menu. Many of the recipes have been with the restaurant for decades. With such a culinary and cocktail pedigree, it's no surprise that mob bosses from Santo Trafficante Sr. and Jr. to Carlos Marcello and Sam Giancana were fans of the Columbia. For over fifty years, FBI and local law enforcement agents frequently ate there as well, enjoying a good meal as they surveilled dining wiseguys. Though the mob in Tampa has faded, the Columbia remains as popular as ever. Reservations recommended.

CHAPTER 8

Bar Noir

When the well feels a bit dry, I like to be at a bar where there is activity but the music isn't too loud, a place where I can see people interacting but I can also hear a bit of their conversations too...
A place like that is worth its weight in gold, or scotch.

AUTHOR NICHOLAS DENMON

Where you imbibe matters just as much as what you imbibe. Writers of all kinds know that. Crime writers may know it best of all. And where they choose to drink is intricately connected to their work as writers.

"Sometimes, you just want to collect your thoughts and not be bothered," said organized crime fiction author Nicholas Denmon. "These are the times when you sit sipping a scotch on a patio some place and idly watch cars and life pass you by. Sometimes you stare straight into the scotch from a corner, dim-lit booth and contemplate your next scene.

"Other times, the best place can be a venue with a vantage point that helps you generate an idea. For me, when the well feels a bit dry, I like to be at a bar where there is activity but the music isn't too loud, a place where I can see people interacting but I can also hear a bit of their conversations too. I don't need to hear every word the subjects say when I people-watch, just enough to stir the imagination. A place like that is worth its weight in gold, or scotch."

No surprise, the Buffalo-based writer has a go-to bar. "My favorite place to grab a drink, especially beer on tap, is Gordon's on Delaware Avenue. It's just a local neighborhood bar with a jukebox, a four-hour 'happy hour' and fantastic wings. It's open until 4 a.m. six nights a week, which you really can't beat."

The crime writer bar can be a neighborhood dive, a tiki hut on a beach, the fancy restaurant where a writer can observe the comings and goings of intriguing characters. It can be a place where other writers congregate to share stories and keep the literary inspiration alive.

For crime novelist Laura Lippman, bars aren't about inspiration but about relaxing after she's finished a book. And she knows exactly what she wants in a watering hole.

"It is within walking distance of my house. It serves better-than-average white wine for $8 a glass," she said. "And it has the world's greatest pomme frites and/or homemade potato chips served with blue cheese. And maybe a little green salad with olives, pistachios, and onions. Also, a cool mix of nuts, chips, pepitas, like the snacks served at my favorite hotel in Cuernavaca, Mexico." Sadly, this bar only exists in Lippman's thirsty imagination. She writes fiction, after all.

Because writing about outlaws requires research, a crime writer bar can occasionally be the kind of place you pass on an-out-of-the-way road, with a few cars in front, and get the sense that if you ever went in you might not make it out.

NEW YORK CITY

New York City, the national capital of publishing, is, fittingly, filled with writers' bars.

Chumley's

This historic Prohibition-era pub on Bedford Street in Greenwich Village is, as of this writing, closed while the owners deal with permitting issues for a reopening. (The building was damaged in a 2007 wall collapse.) A literary landmark, it bears a plaque from the Friends of Libraries USA celebrating its standing as a meeting place for writers from William Faulkner to Ring Lardner.

More recently, legendary New York City writer Jimmy Breslin frequented Chumley's. The Pulitzer Prize-winning journalist has written extensively about crime and the mob for newspapers and in books. His novel *The Gang that Couldn't Shoot Straight* was reportedly based on the early 1960s Gallo-Profaci war between mob boss Joe Profaci and his loyalists and the Gallo faction led by Crazy Joe Gallo. In *The Good Rat*, Breslin tells the true story of Burton Kaplan, a mob-linked drug trafficker who turned against the Mafia in 2004.

BLACK ASS OF JACK DANIEL'S

2 fingers Jack Daniel's
4 ice cubes
Premium water
Put the ice cubes in a short, high-quality glass. Add the two fingers of Jack. Top off with water. Put on *Songs for Swinging Lovers*, sit back, and pretend you're almost half as cool as Sinatra was.

FRANK SINATRA COCKTAIL

This cocktail was created in Philadelphia.
3 oz. dry gin
¾ oz. blue curaçao
1 oz. sweet-and-sour mix
Add ice to a cocktail shaker. Add ingredients. Shake vigorously for 10 seconds and strain into martini glass. Garnish with a lemon slice.

Elaine's

There have been many venerable writers' hangouts in New York City. And then there was Elaine's. Opened in 1963, the Upper East Side restaurant was a magnet for not only actors and musicians, but many of the city's most accomplished writers. Among them, Gay Talese, author of the 1971 true crime masterpiece *Honor Thy Father*, a gripping account of the Bonnano crime family war (dubbed the Banana War by the press). The restaurant closed following the death in 2010 of its proprietor, Elaine Kaufman, the woman who turned it into a writer's clubhouse.

"She made it known to us that she welcomed us. Those of us in journalism, or magazine writing, or book writing weren't exactly sought after by restaurateurs of our youth back in the 1960s," Talese said. "There are people whose personality is so commanding over what they own that without them there is nothing worth owning. And this was true of Elaine's."

Two other crime-writing heavyweights—Peter Maas and Mario Puzo—were regular patrons, soaking up the literary vibe and mixing with the occasional mobster.

In 1968, Maas set the standard for nonfiction books about turncoat mobsters with *The Valachi Papers*, a revealing look at the Mafia through the eyes of former Genovese crime family member Joe Valachi. Maas returned to writing about organized crime snitches for his 1998 book, *Underboss: Sammy the Bull Gravano's Story of Life in the Mafia*.

Mario Puzo, of course, wrote the crime fiction magnum opus, *The Godfather*. One night, after the release of the iconic film adaptation, Frank Sinatra came into Elaine's. He was not happy with Puzo's character Johnny Fontaine. Sinatra felt, and rightfully so, that Fontaine was a thinly veiled caricature of the Hoboken Kid. Elaine tried to get Sinatra to sit down and have a drink with Puzo, who was at a nearby table. Sinatra reportedly refused, had a drink, and left.

Well, anyway, that's one version of what happened. Puzo recalls the night differently.

"Time has mercifully dimmed the humiliation of what followed. Sinatra started to shout abuse. I remember that, contrary to his reputation, he did not use foul language at all," Puzo said. "The worst thing he called me was a pimp. I do remember him saying that if I wasn't so much older than he, he would beat the hell out of me." Puzo said that as he walked out of the restaurant, Sinatra yelled after him, "Choke. Go ahead and choke."

Now that's the Old Blue Eyes we all know and love.

Black Ass of Jack Daniel's

Sinatra, like the rest of the Rat Pack, enjoyed a libation from time to time (okay, all of the time). He loved wine and martinis, but his standby was Jack Daniel's, prepared a specific way, which he called the Black Ass of Jack Daniel's. Frank loved Jack Daniel's so much that the company released a special edition Jack Daniel's Sinatra Select.

P.J. Clarke's

P.J. Clarke's has been a haven for movie stars, musicians, writers, and the occasional gangster. The place is cramped and cluttered, but in a warm and inviting way, from the dark wood bars to the walls covered with photos of former patrons. It's been a staple on the New York cocktail scene for over 100 years. It even has a great gangster story associated with it. According to *The Lufthansa Heist,* a book on the infamous 1978 robbery, mobster Henry Hill (of *Goodfellas* fame) and some associates decided to rob the New York townhome of Estée Lauder. They bound her and started ransacking the apartment. Hill noticed she was convulsing in fear so he offered to take her out. They went for cocktails at P.J. Clarke's while his crew robbed her house.

The bar was also a favorite hangout for some of the writers on *The Sopranos,* including Matthew Weiner, who went on to create *Mad Men*. Weiner sat for a short interview with *The New Yorker* at

Clarke's after the premiere of *Mad Men*, one of the chief pop-culture touchstones for the resurgence of classic cocktails.

THE ALGONQUIN HOTEL COCKTAIL

1½ oz. rye whiskey
¾ oz. dry vermouth
¾ oz. pineapple juice
Add ingredients into a cocktail shaker with ice. Some recipes say shake, others say stir, so you'll have to make two to determine which is best for your palate. Strain into a chilled cocktail glass.

The Algonquin Hotel

One of New York's most storied writer's meeting places is the Algonquin Hotel on Manhattan's West 44th Street. Its then-owner, Frank Case, closed the Algonquin's bar in 1917 and the hotel remained dry through Prohibition. But that didn't stop it from becoming inexorably tied to the American literary scene with the start of the Algonquin Round Table in 1919. This group of writers and critics who met to trade witticisms over lunch included such luminaries as Dorothy Parker, Robert Benchley, Alexander Woollcott, George S. Kaufman, and Harold Ross.

Another writer with a seat at the Round Table was Ring Lardner. He wrote mainly about sports, including the infamous Black Sox scandal of the 1919 World Series, where the White Sox were accused of fixing the series against Cincinnati in a scheme that allegedly involved New York mobster Arnold Rothstein.

Ring also wrote fictional short stories, including "Champion," the portrait of the brutal life of a boxer and corruption in the sport.

Kirk Douglas starred in the 1949 film noir based on the story. The movie version added more organized crime influence and a femme fatale, but maintained the gritty feel of the original story.

Round Table regular and playwright Robert E. Sherwood also penned work with a noir bent. One of his most famous plays, *The Petrified Forest*, was made into a movie in 1936 that is considered one of the earliest film noirs. Humphrey Bogart starred in both the stage and screen adaptations. Sherwood based the main villain, Duke Mantee, on real-life bank robber and gangster John Dillinger.

Most of us would have to rob a bank to afford one of the Algonquin's signature cocktails, a $10,000 martini. The key ingredient, aside from gin, is a diamond resting at the bottom of the glass. If you'd prefer to keep your bar tab below five figures, try The Algonquin Hotel Cocktail. This cocktail was invented, so the story goes, in the early years of the Algonquin Round Table. Even though the hotel was dry, that didn't stop writers from occasionally bringing in booze and creating a cocktail of their own.

New York also has many excellent cocktail lounges that, while not known as crime writer bars, are favorites of another kind of

PEGU CLUB COCKTAIL

This recipe is featured in Harry Craddock's 1930 *Savoy Cocktail Book*. Craddock describes it as "the favorite cocktail of the Pegu Club, Burma, and one that has traveled, and is asked for, round the world."

1½ oz. dry gin
⅔ oz. curaçao
1 tsp. lime juice
1 dash orange bitters
1 dash Angostura bitters
Shake well and strain into cocktail glass.

scribe—those who write about spirits. In some cases they deserve to be considered noir bars because of their cool, dark vibe. In some cases, they're just too good to be ignored on any tour of great cocktail places. If crime writers haven't discovered them yet, they should. So should anyone who enjoys a well-crafted drink or noir story.

Asked his favorite New York City drinks destination, cocktail writer Fredo Ceraso struggled to narrow the list. "I love so many. Sometimes I want a no-frills dive like Jimmy's Corner in Midtown, sometimes fancy world-class joints like Death & Company or The Dead Rabbit, sometimes a neighborhood cocktail den like the Long Island Bar in Brooklyn or Ward 3 in Tribeca."

Spirits writer Kara Newman is "a sucker for hotel bars with history. I especially love the Bemelmans Bar at the Carlyle and the bar in the refurbished Palm Court in the Plaza. That said, I'm still mourning the loss of the venerable Oak Room/Oak Bar at the Plaza. I hope they re-open it soon."

For cocktail guru Dale DeGroff, "In NYC, hands down the best saloon is Hudson and Malone. Pegu Club [on Manhattan's Houston Street] is the best cocktail lounge; you will not get a bad drink. I also like the Clover Club in Brooklyn."

The original Pegu Club was a British gentlemen's club in Burma that opened in the 1880s. It embodied the colonial ambience of a club you'd read about in an Agatha Christie or P.D. James novel.

Its signature drink, the unimaginatively named Pegu Club cocktail, fell out of fashion for decades but is now making a comeback. It's a refreshing, bright cocktail, suitable for the hot, humid tropics of Burma. Or Florida.

AMSTERDAM

Crime writer David Amoruso's favorite bar is in his hometown of Amsterdam. Though he lives in the US now, he remembers frequenting a place at the center of Amsterdam nightlife. Mixed in with the writers were "the city's richest businessmen, famous actors and athletes, who all came here for a drink or bite to eat."

The Café is a crime writer kind of bar, where shady characters hobnob with the elite, and an attentive scribe can pick up snippets of conversation to use in a story. For crime writers like Amoruso, part of the appeal was the Café's underworld clientele, some of the Netherlands' most infamous gangsters. "Men like Johnny Mieremet and Sam Klepper, who were nicknamed Spic & Span for their deadly way of doing business and cleaning up whoever stood in their way. Both men were murdered by assassins; Klepper was killed in 2000 in front of his luxurious Amsterdam apartment, while Mieremet was shot in the head at his office in Pattaya, Thailand in 2005," Amoruso said. "Before their demise, the threesome decided extorting their rich 'friends' at Café Lexington was an easier racket than trafficking drugs, so they plucked millions off frightened Dutch businessmen. It all started, and happened, at Café Lexington."

Heineken Kidnapping

Some of the Café Lexington's regulars were involved in a gangland kidnapping with ties to the liquor industry. The gangsters plotted at the Café to kidnap beer tycoon Freddy Heineken.

"The gangsters behind the kidnapping were all young guys who came from the gritty streets of Amsterdam. While busting heads and hustling tourists they spent the previous two years planning their multi-million-dollar caper," Amoruso said.

On the evening of November 9, 1983, gangsters kidnapped Freddy Heineken and Ab Doderer (his chauffeur) in front of the Heineken office in Amsterdam. They held the men hostage for twenty-one days, until the Heineken family paid a ransom of around $17 million (35 million guilders).

"Unfortunately for the gangsters, the Dutch police were hot on their trail and within four years all but one of the kidnappers were behind bars," Amoruso said. "Around four million dollars of ransom money was never recovered. An informant later told police the money had been buried in a park in Paris, France. After he had dug it up for the group the money was invested in brothels and real estate.

"In the years following the kidnapping, the young gangsters became like folk heroes. The media hounded them, articles and books were written about them, television programs devoted to them, and in recent years two movies were made about the kidnapping, one in the Netherlands and another in Hollywood starring Sir Anthony Hopkins as Heineken."

LOS ANGELES

Musso & Frank Grill

The Musso & Frank Grill, located at 6667 Hollywood Boulevard, has been serving crime writers (as well as movie stars and politicians) since 1919. Dashiell Hammett imbibed while belly up to the small bar. William Faulkner, who wrote the screenplay for the noir classic *The Big Sleep*, was also a regular.

Raymond Chandler was such a fixture there they named a booth after him. In 2012, the Grill held an event celebrating Chandler's work, featuring author John Buntin, who wrote *LA Noir: The Struggle for the Soul of America's Most Seductive City*.

Bestselling crime writer Michael Connelly, author of the Harry Bosch series of books, told *The Guardian*, "If you want a really good drink go to the bar at The Musso & Frank Grill for a martini. It's on Hollywood Boulevard, where it has been for nearly 100 years, and some of the waiters look like they've been there the whole time. It's not big—10 stools at the most. You'll be sitting where Charlie Chaplin sat—it has history."

SAN FRANCISCO

San Francisco has a distinct noir quality that inspired authors for decades. But noir expert Eddie Muller laments the current state of the city's cocktail scene.

"Sadly, I must report that many of the classic spots are closing, or, in many cases, being replaced by trendier versions which are loud, crowded, and absurdly overpriced. The recent 'renaissance' of cocktail culture is great in that it's sparked a new generation's interest in what I'll call the 'art of drinking,' but it's totally missed the easy sophistication that used to be part and parcel of cocktail lounges before they became 'Cocktail Culture.'

"I've always considered the perfect cocktail lounge to be a place of sanctuary; it needed to be either convivial or clandestine. These places used to be everywhere in San Francisco, neighborhood saloons where you strike up a conversation and share drinks with folks from all walks of life, from blue-collar bars to posh hotel bars like the Redwood Room."

Muller added, "But let's face it—even if I found the perfect new cocktail bar I wouldn't tell you about it."

VIEUX CARRÉ

As it says on the Carousel Bar menu, "This signature cocktail of the famous Carousel Bar was first mixed by Walter Berferon in 1938."

¾ oz. rye
¾ oz. cognac
¾ oz. sweet vermouth
1 tsp. Benedictine liqueur
1 dash Peychaud's bitters
1 dash Angostura bitters

Combine ingredients in mixing glass with ice. Stir and strain into rocks glass with ice, or chilled cocktail glass with no ice. Garnish with a lemon peel.

Well, fine. You can, nevertheless, still find vestiges of San Francisco's literary noir past, most associated with Dashiell Hammett. The Garden Court Restaurant in the Palace Hotel was a lunch stop for Hammett's Sam Spade, despite a grand elegance that suggests the stylish Nick and Nora Charles more than the world-weary Spade.

NEW ORLEANS

Carousel Bar

The Carousel Bar, located in the French Quarter, is one of the more well-known drinking establishments in a city famous for drinking establishments. Located in the Hotel Monteleone, it is an actual carousel that rotates slowly (or maybe not so slowly by the third round) and offers a thoughtful menu of classic and signature cocktails.

Dale DeGroff likes the Carousel, "for Marvin Allen (bartender) and because everybody stops at the Carousel." Hemingway mentions the hotel in one of his stories, as do Tennessee Williams and Rebecca Wells. Many of those authors stayed at the hotel, and it's a regular haunt for Southern writers looking for inspiration.

Truman Capote, who wrote the 1966 true crime classic *In Cold Blood*, claimed to have been birthed in one of the rooms at the Hotel Monteleone (he wasn't, but it makes a good story). Erle Stanley Gardner, best known for his pulp crime and Perry Mason novels, also featured the hotel in his books, including *Owls Don't Blink*, a noirish tale set in New Orleans.

KEY WEST

Key West's bar scene is typically associated with either Ernest Hemingway or hordes of drunken college kids on Spring Break. But it's also inspired many writers and artists (e.g. Jimmy Buffett). Mystery author Lisa Unger's favorite bar is in Key West.

"I wouldn't say that I have a regular bar that I visit. But I do have some all-time favorites. Top of the list would have to be Sloppy Joe's in Key West, mainly because it's where I met my husband Jeffrey. It was Ernest Hemingway's favorite haunt toward the end of his life, so there's a literary connection." After meeting her husband, Unger moved from New York City to Florida, where her writing career took off.

Unger's other favorite bars also have a Hemingway connection. "La Bodeguita del Medio in Prague was our favorite spot when we were visiting that beautiful city. It was loud, fun, and full of a wild energy. Papa apparently spent a lot of time there drinking mojitos.

"Bar Hemingway at The Ritz in Paris is a small, discreet, beautiful little spot. It's quite possibly the most expensive bar in the world but worth every penny for the stellar ambiance and delectable cocktails. Visit and you'll know why Hemingway said: *When I dream of an afterlife in heaven, the action always takes place in the Paris Ritz.*"

TAMPA AND ST. PETERSBURG

Crime writer bars in the Tampa Bay area tend not to have the historic cachet of those in some other parts of the country (though, if you want to talk other types of writers, Jack Kerouac lived in St. Petersburg for a time and frequented the Flamingo Sports Bar on 9th Street N.). For decades the neighborhood corner bar was about as fancy as you could find. Journalists who covered crime for the local papers would gather at places like The Hub in downtown Tampa or Mastry's in St. Petersburg, both still around, and both about as awesomely divvy as you can get. What better place to muse on crime than in a dingy, smoky, old man bar, elbow to elbow with characters that you won't find at a fancy hotel lounge.

Of late, the area's cocktail scene has been changing. As sommelier and wine writer Erin Kane explained, "There are several that now offer a more creative cocktail experience than your average Tampa Bay establishment. For example Anise, in downtown Tampa, crafts innovative drinks that play with your senses—go and try the 'Gin Sing.' Newer to the scene is Ulele, which also has an imaginative drink menu."

Having made Florida my home for the past 20 years, I naturally have a few favorite bars in Tampa and St. Petersburg. My Tampa choices include King Corona Cigars in Ybor City. It only serves beer and wine, but it's the best place to get a great brew and match it with a fine cigar. King Corona has the feel of an old Ybor place, where the bolita throwers and gangsters would hang out smoking cigars and drinking café con leche. I'm also a fan of Fly Bar in downtown Tampa, one of the first craft cocktail bars in the downtown area. It has a long menu of traditional and modern cocktail creations. The bartenders are knowledgeable and keep their heads, even during the happy-hour crush.

Tampa-based wine and spirits writer Erin Kane. Photo credit: Erin Kane.

The spot that really ties into my crime writing is at The Columbia Restaurant. It's a fantastic old bar, in a side room of the restaurant. It's open and airy, comfortable. The cocktails are classic and well made. It's the place where local wiseguys would have deviled crab (a Tampa specialty—crab meat and Cuban bread deep fried. Basically a gigantic crab cake, but so much more) while drinking sangria or a mojito, and entertain visiting mobsters from around the country.

In St. Petersburg, there is the site of the old Gangplank speakeasy, at 1700 Park Boulevard N., on the west side of town. It's had several restaurants and bar iterations throughout the years, and as of this writing is currently vacant. But there was a bar there that dated back to the 1920s and was a hangout for Al Capone when he visited St. Petersburg during spring training. I always got the Capone-era vibe from the bar.

Most of my favorite St. Pete bars (Mandarin Hide, The Emerald) are not directly tied to writing but enjoyable gathering spots with exceptional drinks.

The one watering hole that inspires me the most and serves my writing is my home bar. It's the place where I can try new libations inspired by my writing, or take a break when writer's block sets in. It's not fancy, but decently well stocked (consider this foreshadowing for Chapter 9) and just a few feet away. No car required.

BEACH BARS

Beach bars dot most coastal communities, but are especially popular in tropical areas like Florida, California, Hawaii, and the Caribbean. While beach bars don't have the dark, gritty allure of city bars, they are a haven for all sorts of nefarious characters and the authors who chronicle their exploits. Sure, beach bars often get overrun by tourists. But that makes them good hunting grounds for con men and pickpockets. The large crowd could be just what an outlaw needs to blend in when discussing drug-smuggling schemes. And high-end beach bars are often portrayed as the hangouts of warm-weather gangland bosses. How many movies and books have a poolside scene with the criminal flanked by beautiful bikini-clad women, sipping on a cocktail (often rum-based)?

Florida Noir author Bob Morris has a list of favorite beach bars that he likes to visit, lingering a while and drawing inspiration for his next novel.

Maui: Merriman's.

Coconut Grove: Scotty's (although it's more of a marina)

Jost Van Dyke: Sydney's Peace and Love

Nevis: Sunshine's

Elbow Cay: Abaco Inn

Great Abaco: Pete's Pub

Harbour Island: Sip-Sip

Stocking Island, Exuma: Chat 'n' Chill

FLORIDA TRACK SUIT

½ oz. orange vodka
½ oz. raspberry liqueur
2 oz. Red Bull

Combine the vodka and liqueur in a small glass. Add to a glass of the Red Bull and shoot it down.

RUM RUNNER

2 cups ice
1 oz. pineapple juice
1 oz. orange juice
1 oz. blackberry liqueur
1 oz. banana liqueur
1 oz. light rum
1 oz. dark rum or aged rum
Splash grenadine
Optional: 1 oz. of Bacardi 151 to float on top
Orange slice (optional)

You can find the Rum Runner as a blended drink: Fill blender with ice. Add all ingredients and blend until smooth. Pour into hurricane-style glass and garnish with orange and float of 151.

Or you can make it on the rocks: Fill glass with ice. Add all ingredients and stir. Pour 151 in the straw and drink up!

BLUE OCEAN

1 oz. vodka
½ oz. blue curaçao
⅓ oz. grapefruit juice
¼ oz. simple syrup
Add all ingredients to a shaker filled with ice. Shake vigorously, then strain into large glass with ice. Garnish with orange, pineapple, or other tropical fruit.

MAI TAI

¾ oz. dark rum
1 oz. light rum
½ oz. orgeat syrup
½ oz. Cointreau
½ oz. lime juice
½ oz. simple syrup
Add ingredients in a cocktail shaker with ice and shake vigorously for 30 seconds. Serve in a large glass with crushed ice. Garnish with a cherry.

Green Turtle Cay: Sundowner's
Santa Barbara: Brophy's.
New Smyrna Beach: Tony & Joe's.
St. Martin: Karackter.

One of my favorite beach bars is the Undertow on St. Pete Beach. Over the past few years it has gotten a little too crowded and popular for its own good, but it's still a must visit for newcomers to the west coast of Florida. Along the Pinellas County coast are a number of small tiki-hut-style bars, often attached to hotels, that invariably feature a guy playing Jimmy Buffett and classic rock cover songs on an acoustic guitar, serving simple cold beer selections and if you're lucky some good fried grouper.

Right now, with the resurgence of classic cocktail lounges, beach bars are upping their game and moving away from syrupy pre-mixed cocktails towards more authentic tiki drinks, as well as other lighter cocktails to imbibe in the hot sun.

Florida Track Suit

This concoction (more accurately, a shot) was actually created in Canada, but its name evokes the stereotypical old New Yorker hanging out in the beach bars of South Florida, wearing a polyester track suit, unbuttoned to his navel. However, the drink, heavy with Red Bull, was probably gunning for a younger demographic.

Boca Cocktail

Not a cocktail but a slang term for water with lemon ordered by elderly customers at restaurants in South Florida. When ordered (free of charge) and mixed with sugar, it serves as a reasonable lemonade substitute and doesn't cost a thing.

Rum Runner

The Rum Runner is a true Floridian cocktail, created in the 1950s at the Holiday Isle Tiki Bar in Islamorada, one of the Florida Keys. At the time, the bartender had an excess of rum and other liqueurs and created this drink to use them up. At least that's the legend. Problem was the Tiki Bar didn't exist back then. The place was operating under a different name. Another origin story has the drink created in the 1970s. But spirits historian Dr. Ron A. Nejo said he couldn't find any mention of the drink from bartending books of that time.

All we do know for sure is that it's now a staple of Florida beach bars. And it's delicious.

Blue Ocean

One of the most vibrantly colored cocktails you'll find, it's also relatively easy to make for your own poolside enjoyment. The deep blue color comes from blue curaçao. This liqueur is made on the island of curaçao and flavored with laraha, a citrus fruit found only on the island.

Mai Tai

A staple of the tiki lounge craze from the 1950s, the mai tai is a popular beach bar libation, featuring that most tropical of spirits, rum.

NEW ENGLAND

Congress Street Bar and Grill

Congress Street Bar and Grill in Portland, Maine is a favorite for crime author Dick Cass. He likes "its neighborhood love, its limited seating, and the fine feeling of having your drink order remembered almost as soon as you walk in."

J.J. Foleys

Foley's, on E. Berkeley Street, has been an Irish pub standby in the neighborhood since 1909. It's a popular gathering place for Boston-area journalists and writers, as the *Boston Herald*'s offices are nearby. During Prohibition the pub supposedly fronted as a shoe store and served drinks in the back.

The Bar at Taj Boston

This bar has been around since 1927 and hosted many famous guests over the years. Though not necessarily a haunt of crime writers, it was a place for poets like Sylvia Plath and Anne Sexton to "talk of poetry and suicide attempts over martinis and free potato chips."

The Cop Bar

When Brian Thiem turned to writing crime fiction, he had an advantage over most newcomers—twenty-five years of experience on the Oakland Police Department. For other crime writers, the next best source of material might be hanging out in a cop bar. Asked what makes a good bar, Thiem had a ready list of criteria.

"Close to and accessible to the police station: It's got to be easy for cops to stop by when they get off work. Over the years, there've been a number of different watering holes frequented by OPD. When I came on, the old-timers went to a bar that was within a Hofbrau right across the street from the PAB (Police Administration Building), but the place closed in the late '80s. The younger officers started going to a bar in a Mexican restaurant a block away. Vice Narcotics and Intel (the undercover cops of the department) drank at a small, dark hotel bar across the street from the PAB. These guys couldn't hang out with the regular cops if they were to maintain their covers. The Warehouse began transitioning to *the* cop bar in the late '80s and has been so ever since. It's four blocks away with plenty of on-street parking.

"Cop-friendly management and bartenders: They either encourage or discourage cops to frequent the place; there's no in-between. Sometimes a place might be a cop bar and then management changes and tries to attract a more upscale clientele, so the cops drift away. It wouldn't be a place for ACLU attorneys or public defenders, but many prosecutors from the DA's office would be seen there. Non-affiliated women who come to The Warehouse like cops; the term 'police-groupie' seems too disrespectful.

"Cheap drinks: It doesn't have to be the cheapest place in town, but most cops aren't interested in $10 martinis or $12 shots of top-shelf tequila. They're more likely to drink domestic beer (out of the bottle or by the pitcher) and simple mixed drinks. Free happy-hour food is another plus.

"A sense of community: A good cop bar is like an old-time neighborhood bar, only the neighborhood is mostly occupied by cops and their friends. Cops feel safe and comfortable there, and everyone knows one another. Several years after I quit drinking, I returned to The Warehouse for a fellow officer's retirement party one night. It was the first time I'd been there in years, but before I got halfway across the room, the bartender had an open bottle of Bud Light on the bar waiting for me along with a 'How ya doing, Brian.' It was as if I'd just been there the night before. It's where cops go to celebrate or mourn."

CHAPTER 9

The Well-Stocked Home Bar

It all starts with the ingredients. Fresh fruits and high-quality mixers make the difference between a so-so cocktail and one that you or your guests will rave about. The following is a list, though by no means a complete list, of spirits, mixers, and other ingredients featured in the cocktails in this book. There are hundreds of other cocktail ingredients available, some regional, some obscure. But the ones here should be familiar to any home mixologist.

Add even a few, and you'll be ready to mix superb classic cocktails at home. Serve them while you're hosting gangsters, femme fatales, and other friends. Fix yourself an old-school cocktail to sip as you soak in a Bogie-and-Bacall film noir or hardboiled Raymond Chandler novel.

As noted throughout *Cocktail Noir*, many "classic" drinks lend themselves to numerous variations, and taste can be as individual as the fingerprints on a smoking revolver. So feel free to experiment. Just don't think of making an appletini. That would be a crime.

Absinthe—The fabled green dragon that inspired the Impressionists and was known for its hallucinogenic properties was not available in the United States for many years. In the last five years it has become easier to find not only European absinthe, but some domestic brands as well. Absinthe, a key ingredient in a Sazerac, has a strong anise flavor. And while the psychotropic effects of the drink have been exaggerated, it packs quite a punch.

Aperitif—An aperitif is a spirit consumed before a meal to stimulate the appetite. Most have a bitter quality. Popular aperitifs include vermouth, Campari, and Dubonnet.

Benedictine—This French herbal liqueur is a blend of twenty-seven plants and spices including aloe and cinnamon. It's sweet yet herbal and has a strong flavor profile.

Bitters—Bitters are essential ingredients in so many cocktails. Alcohol infused with a variety of herbs and spices, bitters can liven up and add depth to cocktails.

Blue Curaçao—Curaçao is a liqueur flavored with lahara fruit, bitter versions of Valencia oranges that were brought by the Spanish to the island of Curaçao. Thought the flesh is inedible, the peel releases a flowery fragrance. The liqueur can be found in a few colors, though blue is the most common for cocktails.

Crème de Cacao—The ultimate in dessert libations, this chocolate liqueur can be consumed straight as an after-dinner drink or mixed in a sweet cocktail. It's also featured in many dessert recipes.

Cynar—This artichoke-based bitter liqueur can be either an aperitif or a digestif.

Digestif—These spirits are consumed after dinner to aid in digestion. Unlike aperitifs with their bitter quality, digestifs tend to be on the sweeter side. Cognac is a popular digestif, as are port and Limoncello. Grappa, Sambuca, and aquavits are more robust digestifs, while my personal favorite, Fernet Branca, belongs to a bitter digestif family. Fernet is not for the unadventurous.

Dubonnet—This aperitif was originally created to make quinine more palatable to French Foreign Legion officers stationed in Africa. The concoction was developed by a pharmacist, Joseph Dubonnet. Quinine was the extract of the cinchona bark, and used to combat malaria.

Grenadine—Bottled grenadine syrup is very sweet and very red. It's an ingredient in that most classic of cocktails, the Shirley Temple. But real grenadine can be made at home and is superior to the high-sugar pre-made mixer. There are many recipes available. This one is from *Chow*.

GRENADINE

1 cup pomegranate juice
1 cup granulated sugar
¼ teaspoon lemon juice
2–3 drops orange-flower water

Heat pomegranate juice in small saucepan over medium heat until steam rises. Remove from heat. Add sugar and stir until it dissolves and is no longer cloudy (about 5 minutes). Stir in lemon juice and orange-flower water and let the syrup cool to room temperature, about 40 minutes. Transfer to a container with a tight-fitting lid and refrigerate for up to 1 month.

Lillet—Lillet is an aperitif wine from France. It's from Pondesac, a region of Bordeaux. It can be imbibed straight (it should be chilled). But it's also an excellent cocktail mixer. The main varieties are Lillet Blanc, Lillet Rouge, and the newer Lillet Rose.

Maraschino Cherry Liqueur—This essential bar ingredient is made from Marasca cherries, a sour variety found in Croatia. The cherries are distilled and combined with sugar before bottling. A slightly bitter and sweet flavor was popular in a number of classic cocktails, including the Aviation and the Martinez. It has enjoyed a resurgence in recent years.

Maraschino Cherries—These sweet, candied cherries are often associated with sugar and bright red dyed varieties that are as at home on top of a sundae as they are in a cocktail.

Bada Bing Cherries—These artisanal maraschino cherries in syrup are available online from Tillen Farms. In February of 2015, Arthur Mondella, operator of a large maraschino cherry factory in Brooklyn, killed himself as police were raiding the factory and uncovering a massive marijuana-growing operation in the factory's basement.

Orange Liqueur—Any well-stocked bar should have at least one kind of orange liqueur. They are flavorful and flexible, and add a variety of touches and finishes to cocktails. Many orange liqueurs are referred to as "triple sec." Triple sec is similar to curaçao but has a sweeter flavor due to the type of oranges used.

Cointreau—Probably one of the better-known orange liqueurs, Cointreau was first distilled in France in 1875. It has a powerful bittersweet orange flavor that can be overwhelming if not added correctly to cocktails.

Grand Marnier—This blend of cognac and oranges also dates back to France in the late 1800s. It can be enjoyed both on the rocks and in cocktails.

Orgeat Syrup—Orgeat syrup, a sweet almond syrup with orange-flower water is a key ingredient in many tiki-themed cocktails, from the Mai-Tai to the Stinger. Now made with an emulsion of almonds, giving it a milk-like appearance and viscosity, the syrup can be traced back to the 1300s when it was made with barley. The almond style can be found in cocktail recipes from the 1860s. But the ingredient became ubiquitous in cocktail culture when it was used as a sweetener in various tiki concoctions starting in the 1950s. However, it's still relatively unknown to the general drinking populace.

Rose's Lime Cordial—Essential for a gimlet, this lime juice/sugar mix brings out the gimlet flavor better than fresh lime juice. But for all other cocktails using lime, fresh is always best.

Sambuca—Sambuca is an anise-flavored liqueur. Though it comes in a few varieties, white Sambuca is the most popular.

ORGEAT SYRUP

This recipe is from *Punch* magazine. You can find other recipes online with varying degrees of difficulty.

1 pound bitter almonds*
3 cups water
3 cups sugar
1 teaspoon salt
1 teaspoon rosewater
1 tablespoon orange-blossom water

In a pan over medium-low heat, toast the almonds until the oils begin to release, and a light color has been achieved.

Add the almonds to a large Ziploc bag containing the water. Hack sous vide: Set a colander or a steaming basket inside a larger pot of water set over the lowest heat possible. Drop the bag inside the colander (it should be completely submerged), and cook in the hot water bath for 4 hours. Strain and discard the almonds, reserving the warm liquid. Add sugar and salt, and stir to dissolve. Seal in an airtight container, allow to come to room temperature and then cool in the refrigerator. Add the rosewater and orange-blossom water to finish. Store, refrigerated, in an airtight container for up to 2 weeks.

**When sourcing bitter almonds, look for something labeled as "bitter almond seeds," which are opaque and white. Your best bet is an Asian or Middle Eastern grocery.*

Simple Syrup—This is one of the easiest cocktail ingredients to make by yourself. There are bottled versions available, but there is really no reason not to make this at home.

Vermouth—Vermouth is a fortified wine that originated in Italy. It's an essential ingredient in a variety of cocktails. Vermouth can be used in cooking as well, substituting for wine. There are many different varieties of vermouth, as well as brands. Most vermouth comes from France or Italy, though there have been some American-made ones in recent years.

Dry Vermouth—Predominately from France, this white vermouth is most often associated with the martini. It gives a dry, nuanced flavor that pairs well with other clear spirits.

Sweet Vermouth—Made mainly in Italy, sweet vermouth can be imbibed on the rocks, with soda, or as an ingredient in many cocktails, like the Manhattan.

SIMPLE SYRUP

Equal parts sugar and water.

Boil sugar and water together until sugar dissolves (about five minutes). Cool completely and put in mason jar or other glass container. Store in refrigerator for up to a month.

Acknowledgements

First, as always, I'd like to thank my family for all their support (and patience!) during the writing of another book.

Big thanks are nowhere near enough for the best agent in the world, Gina Panettieri, whose hard work, support, and initial idea for a cocktail-themed book helped bring *Cocktail Noir* to fruition

This book would also not be possible without the amazing staff at Reservoir Square Books—Karen Holt, Simone Skeen, Paul Harrington, and Paul Myatovich. And kudos to the hard work of publicist extraordinaire Michelle Blankenship for taking the book's marketing to the next level (and them some)

Thanks to Phil Samano (@classiclasvegas) for the excellent vintage Vegas material; Christian Cipollini for the photos and the interview; Jonathan Ullman, Geoff Schumacher, Ashley Erickson, Ashley Misko, and the rest of The Mob Museum staff; Lisa Figueredo at Tampamafia.com; Gary Rappaport, Mike Merino, and Sandi Lanksy; Jon Hull and Karen Farb (for overall cocktail support); Jason Wilson, whose book *Boozehound* really took my general interest in cocktails to the next level; all the bartenders and mixologists I've met while researching the book and helped to expand my knowledge of spirits and libations, and a big thanks to Keith Baker for testing out the Cocktail Noir cocktail. Next one's on me Keith.

And finally a tip of the hat to all the interviewees who were gracious enough to allow me to pester them about what and where they like to drink: T.J. English, Dennis Lehane, Bob Morris, Lisa Unger, Michele Dorsey, Dick Cass, Eddie Muller, Laura Lippman, Lisa Unger, Scott M. Burnstein, Kate Flora, Nicholas Denmon, Patrick Downey, Frank Hayde, Oscar Goodman, Dave Karraker, Sonny Girard, Frank Calabrese Jr., Jack Falcone, John Alite, Steve Lenehan, Dale DeGoff, Kara Newman, Derek Brown, Robert Simonson, Fredo Ceraso, Seth Ferranti, Chriss Lyon, Gavin Schmitt, Erin Kane, Brian Thiem, Joel Catanzaro, Dave Jemilo, and David Amoruso.

As always, there are probably a few more people I forgot to thank. This time I have a really good excuse—the cocktails!

References

Books

Brown, Jared and Anistatia Miller. 2011. *The Mixellany Guide to Vermouth & Other Aperitifs*. Cheltenham, UK: Mixellany Limited

Cain, James M. 2003. *The Postman Always Rings Twice, Double Indemnity, and Selected Stories*. New York: Everyman's Library.

Chandler, Raymond. 1992. *The Long Goodbye*. New York: First Vintage Crime. (Reprint.)

Craddock, Harry. 1930. *The Savoy Cocktail Book*. Girard & Stewart.

Crumley, James. 1975. *The Wrong Case*. New York: Random House.

DeGroff, Dale. 2002. *The Craft of the Cocktail: Everything You Need to Know to be a Master Bartender, with 500 Recipes*. New York: Clarkson Potter.

Deitche, Scott and Ken Sanz. 2009. *Balls: The Life of Eddie Trascher, Gentleman Gangster*. Fort Lee, NJ: Barricade Books.

Drury, John. 1931. *Dining in Chicago*. New York: The John Day Company.

Duncan, Paul and Steve Schapiro. 2013. *The Godfather Family Album*. New York: Taschen.

English, T.J. 1990. *The Westies*. New York: St. Martins Paperback.

Fleming, Ian. 2012. *Casino Royale*. Seattle: Thomas and Mercer. (Reprint.)

Hammett, Dashiell. 1989. *The Thin Man*. New York: Vintage. (Reprint.)

Herschlag, Rich and Tony DelVecchio. 2011. *Sinatra, Gotti, and Me: The Rise and Fall of Jilly's Nightclub*. New York: ArcheBooks.

Hortis, C. Alexander. 2014. *The Mob and the City: The Hidden History of How the Mafia Captured New York*. New York: Prometheus.

Johnson, Harry. 1934. *Harry Johnson's Bartenders Manual*. Newark, NJ: Charles E. Graham & Co.

Lehr, Dick and Gerard O'Neil. 2001. *Black Mass: The True Story of an Unholy Alliance Between the FBI and the Irish Mob*. New York: Perennial.

Mosley, Walter. 2010. *Black Betty*. New York: Simon and Schuster Digital. (Reprint.)

Rippetoe, Rita Elizabeth. 2004. *Booze and the Private Eye: Alcohol in the Hard-Boiled Novel*. Jefferson, NC: McFarland & Company.

Thomas, Jerry. 1887. *The Bar-Tenders Guide, or How to Mix All Kinds of Plain and Fancy Drinks*. New York: Dick & Fitzgerald.

Widdicombe, Toby. 2001. *A Reader's Guide to Raymond Chandler*. Santa Barbara, CA: Greenwood. https://books.google.com/books

Willet, Andrew. 2013. *Elemental Mixology*. Raleigh, NC: Lulu.

Wilson, Jason. 2001. *Boozehound: On the Trail of the Rare, the Obscure, and the Overrated in Spirits*. Berkley: Ten Speed Press.

Articles

Ralph Blumenthal, "Look Who Dropped In At the Stork," *New York Times*, July 1, 1996, http://www.nytimes.com/1996/07/01/nyregion/look-who-dropped-in-at-the-stork.html

Fredo Ceraso, "Happy Hour: The Westie Cocktail," *Umani Mart*, April 3, 2012, accessed on March 3, 2015, http://blog.umamimart.com/2012/04/happy-hour-the-westie-cocktail/

Josh Childs, "Scotch Cocktails with Cutty Sark," *boston.com*, December 6,

2012, accessed on September 12, 2014, http://www.boston.com/lifestyle/food/blogs/cocktail/2012/12/scotch_cocktails_with_cutty_sark.html

Ashley Jude Collie, "Vincent Piazza Gets Lucky," *Made Men*, September 4, 2014, accessed September 8, 2014, http://www.mademan.com/boardwalk-empires-vincent-piazza-gets-lucky/#ixzz3Cq4GJrEi

Manny Fernandez, "Onetime Mob Stronghold Hears Echoes of the Old Days," *New York Times*, June 11, 2007, http://www.nytimes.com/2007/06/11/nyregion/11bensonhurst.html?_r=0

Simon Ford, "How the Prohibition Era Shaped the Way we Drink Today," *Food Republic*, September 27, 2012, accessed March 1, 2015, http://www.foodrepublic.com/2012/09/27/how-the-prohibition-era-shaped-the-way-we-drink-today/

Alex Freeman, "Chicago in the 20s: Eat and Drink Mafia Style." *North By Northwestern*, October 7, 2008, accessed September 18, 2014, http://www.northbynorthwestern.com/story/chicago-in-the-20s-eat-and-drink-mafia-style/

Dwight Garner, "A Critic's Tour of Literary Manhattan," *New York Times*, December 14, 2012, http://www.nytimes.com/2012/12/16/travel/a-critics-tour-of-literary-manhattan.html

J. David, Gonzalez, "Noir Flourishes in the Sunshine State," *Salon*, July 26, 2013, accessed September 14, 2014, http://www.salon.com/2013/07/26/give_florida_credit_for_its_crime_novels_partner/

Robert Hull, "Best-selling Crime Novelist Michael Connelly on Los Angeles," *The Guardian*, October 27, 2014, http://www.theguardian.com/travel/2014/oct/27/los-angeles-michael-connelly

Kristin Hunt, "8 Restaurants with Insane Connections to the Mob," *Thril-*

list, accessed September 18, 2014, https://www.thrillist.com/eat/nation/8-restaurants-with-insane-connections-to-the-mob.

August Kleinzahler, "The Inebriate Life / Alcohol Didn't Slow Dashiell Hammett's Profuse Prose," *SFGate*, February 6, 2005, http://www.sfgate.com/magazine/article/The-Inebriate-Life-Alcohol-didn-t-slow-2701044.php

Chantal Martineau, "Our 10 Favorite Prohibition-Era Cocktails to Stir Before Watching Boardwalk Empire," *Food Republic*, September 21, 2012, accessed September 14, 2014, http://www.foodrepublic.com/2012/09/21/our-10-favorite-prohibition-era-cocktails-to-stir-before-watching-boardwalk-empire/.

John Marzulli, "Rat Son Kevin McMahon's Tales of Life with ol "dad' John Carneglia," *New York Daily News*, February 17, 2009, accessed August 30, 2014, http://www.nydailynews.com/news/crimc/rat-son-kevin-mcmahon-tales-life-ol-dad-john-carneglia-article-1.367540#ixzz3C0E1GB8F

Greg Morabito, "The New York Bars and Restaurants of Goodfellas." *New York Eater*, January 18, 2012, accessed September 18, 2014, http://ny.eater.com/maps/the-new-york-bars-and-restaurants-of-goodfellas

Troy Patterson, "The Gimlet Eye: Considering the most unscrewupable of cocktails," *Slate*, December 5, 2013, accessed September 14, 2014, http://www.slate.com/articles/life/drink/2013/12/the_gimlet_a_history_of_gin_and_rose_s_from_the_british_navy_to_raymond.html

Neal Pollack, "The L.A. Noir Tour," *Wall Street Journal*, December 11, 2010, accessed October 4, 2014, http://www.wsj.com/articles/SB10001424052748704156304576003660641749094

Brian Quinn, "Ramos Gin Fizz Recipe," *Food Republic*, August 2, 2012, http://www.foodrepublic.com/recipes/ramos-gin-fizz-recipe/

Selwyn Raab, "Gotti Begins Life Sentence at Prison in Illinois," *New York*

Times, June 25, 1992, accessed February 24, 2015, http://www.nytimes.com/1992/06/25/nyregion/gotti-begins-life-sentence-at-prison-in-illinois.html

William Sertl, "Campari: Good and Bitter," *Saveur*, February 5, 2007, http://www.saveur.com/article/Wine-and-Drink/Campari-Good-and-Bitter

Lucy Shaw, "Top 10 American Gangsters and their Drinks," *The Drinks Business*, April 2, 2014, accessed September 18, 2014, http://www.thedrinksbusiness.com/2014/04/top-10-american-gangsters-and-their-drinks/4/

Patrick Sisson, "An Oral History of the Green Mill," *Chicago Reader*, March 20, 2014, accessed on December 1, 2014, http://www.chicagoreader.com/chicago/uptown-greenmilljazz-bar-history-owner-bartender-musicians/Content?oid=12784766

Gay Talese, "Interview with Gay Talese on the Closing of Elaine's." Interview by KCRW, accessed on December 12, 2014, https://soundcloud.com/kcrw/gay-talese-on-the-closing-of

Wright Thompson, "Four Nights at Elaine's: The Last Will and Testament of a Great Saloon," *Grantland*, June 13, 2011, accessed December 1, 2014, http://grantland.com/features/last-testament-great-saloon/

Adam Tokarz, "History on Tap: A Stumbling Tour of Some of Boston's Famed Watering Holes," *stuffboston.com*, March 9, 2012, http://stuffboston.com/2012/03/13/history-on-tap-a-stumbling-tour-of-some-of-boston%E2%80%99s-storied-watering-holes#.VfGMiWRViko

Bill von Maurer, "Even in Old Days, Sinatra did it his Way." *Palm Beach Post*, September 24, 1988, https://news.google.com/newspapers?nid=1964&dat=19880924&id=xkcjAAAAIBAJ&sjid=r8wFAAAAIBAJ&pg=4046,594434&hl=en

"Goodfellas mobster Henry Hill took cosmetics queen Estee Lauder out for drinks as his 'crew' robbed her New York City townhouse," *Daily Mail*, accessed February 14, 2015, http://www.dailymail.co.uk/news/article-2545862/Goodfellas-mobster-Henry-Hill-took-cosmetics-queen-Estee-Lauder-drinks-crew-robbed-New-York-City-townhouse.html

"Fail to Surrender to Boston Police," The Lewiston Daily Sun, February 3, 1933, https://news.google.com/newspapers?nid=IT5EXw6i2GUC&dat=19330203&printsec=frontpage&hl=en

Law Enforcement Reports

Note on below sources: I utilized over 50 individual memos and filings from the FBI and US Department of Justice. The below sources are aggregates of the individual files.

Federal Bureau of Investigation, Boston Field Office Bureau Airtels, *Memorandums, and Reports 1960–1963*.

Federal Bureau of Investigation, Chicago Field Office Bureau Airtels, *Memorandums, and Reports 1960–1974*.

Federal Bureau of Investigation, "Criminal Influence in Hotels, Motels, and Night Clubs in the Greater Miami Florida Area." Miami, December 23, 1963.

Federal Bureau of Investigation, *ELSUR Logs*, January 1-9, 1964, April 14, 1948.

Federal Bureau of Investigation, Detroit Field Office Bureau Airtels, *Memorandums, and Reports 1958–1964*.

Federal Bureau of Investigation, "Joseph Francis Civello, a.k.a. Anti-Racketeering." Airtel, June 6, 1961.

Federal Bureau of Investigation, Los Angeles Field Office Bureau Airtels, *Memorandum, and Reports, 1960–1970.*

Federal Bureau of Investigation, "Little Rock-Owen Vincent Madden." *Memorandum*, September 23, 1960.

Federal Bureau of Investigation, New York Field Office Bureau Airtels, *Memorandums, and Reports, 1960–1970.*

Federal Bureau of Investigation, Philadelphia Field Office Bureau Airtels, *Memorandum, and Reports, 1960–1970.*

Federal Bureau of Investigation, "Report of Special Agent Richard C. Thompson, Milwaukee Field Office." Milwaukee, December 23, 1963.

Federal Bureau of Investigation, "Sam Saia." *Memorandum*, November 30, 1964.

Federal Bureau of Investigation, "Surveillance of Sam Giancana." Chicago, 1961–1967.

United States Department of Justice, "Crime Survey." March 9, 1944.

United States Department of Justice, "Criminal Influence in the Hotels, Motels, and Night Clubs in the Greater Miami, Florida Area." November 30, 1962.

Websites and Blogs

"10 Awesome Mob Cocktails," Buzzfeed, accessed August 26, 2014, http://www.buzzfeed.com/themobmuseum/10-awesome-mob-cocktails-s0q8

"1950s Cocktail Culture & 1950S Cocktail Recipes," Fifties Wedding, http://fiftieswedding.com/1950s-cocktail-culture-1950s-cocktail-recipes/

"40s Themed Drinks," Midnight Mixologist, accessed November 3, 2014 from http://www.midnightmixologist.com/40s

"Bars and Taverns," Right Here NYC, accessed April 1, 2015, http://righthe-renyc.com/BEEN_HERE_BARS.html

"Cocktail Guide to Film Noir," The Gourmet Detective, accessed September 14, 2014, http://gourmetdetective.com/cocktail-guide-to-film-noir

"Brandy Milk Punch," New Orleans Official Guide, accessed April 7, 2015, http://www.neworleansonline.com/neworleans/cuisine/drinks/bran-dymilkpunch.html?notmct=15

"Chicago Cocktail", Imbibe, accessed February 12, 2015, http://imbibe-magazine.com/recipe-chicago-cocktail/

"Detectives & Their Drink: Cocktail Recipes & Thin Man Martini Video," Mystery Fanfare, http://mysteryreadersinc.blogspot.com/2011/05/de-tectives-their-drink-cocktail-recipes.html

"Floating Through Repeal Day: the Twelve Mile Limit Cocktail," Cold Glass, accessed September 14, 2014, http://cold-glass.com/2011/12/05/float-ing-through-repeal-day-the-twelve-mile-limit-cocktail/

"How to Make a Scofflaw Cocktail," Liquor.com, accessed February 12, 2015, http://liquor.com/video/scofflaw-video/#sM2rcolQW83LswHD.97

"If Walls Could Talk: Mockingbird Hill," Ghosts of DC, accessed March 13, 2015, http://ghostsofdc.org/2013/09/02/walls-talk-mockingbird-hill/

"Left Hand," The Paternal Drunk, accessed October 4, 2014, http://thepa-ternaldrunk.com/2014/09/28/left-hand/

"Lucky Luciano At The Waldorf Astoria: 301 Park Avenue," Infamous New York, http://infamousnewyork.com/

"Mean Streets Cocktail," Imbibe, accessed February 21, 2015, http://im-bibemagazine.com/mean-streets-cocktail-recipe/

"Miss Charming's Silver Screen Cocktails," http://www.miss-charming.com/bartender/silverscreencocktails.html

"Tahiti Bar and Package," Critiki, accessed March 27, 2015, http://critiki.com/location/?loc_id=360

"The Gangster Martini," The Cooking Bride, accessed February 21, 2015, http://cookingbride.com/beverages/the-gangster-martini/

The Pedennis Club, accessed January 13, 2015, http://www.pendennisclub.org/index.html

Index

B

D

E

F

G

H

I

J

M

N

O

P

Q

R

S

T

U

V

W

Y

Z